## EDUCATION MATTERS

General Editor: Professor Ted Wragg

# THE NEW CURRICULUM

# THE NEW CURRICULUM

# CURRICULUM

## Richard Pring

CASSELL

**Cassell Educational Limited**
Artillery House
Artillery Row
London SW1P 1RT

First published 1989

ISBN 0-304-31710-1 (hardback)
0-304-31709-8 (paperback)

**British Library Cataloguing in Publication Data**
Pring, Richard
   The new curriculum.
   1. Great Britain. Schools. Curriculum
   I. Title
   375′.00941

Phototypeset by Input Typesetting Ltd, London

Printed and bound in Great Britain by
Biddles Ltd., Guildford and King's Lynn

# CONTENTS

To Katherine

# FOREWORD

Professor E. C. Wragg, Exeter University

During the 1980s a succession of Education Acts changed considerably the nature of schools and their relationships with the outside world. Parents in particular were given more rights and responsibilities, including the opportunity to serve on the governing body of their child's school. The 1988 Education Reform Act in particular, by introducing for the first time a National Curriculum, the testing of children at the ages of 7, 11, 14 and 16, local management, including financial responsibility and the creation of new types of school, was a radical break with the past.

In the wake of such rapid and substantial changes it was not just parents and lay people, but also teachers and other professionals working in education, who found themselves struggling to keep up with what these many changes meant and how to get the best out of them. The *Education Matters* series addresses directly the major topics of reform, such as the new curriculum, testing and assessment, the role of parents and the handling of school finances, considering their effects on both primary and secondary education.

The aim of the series is to present information about the challenges facing education in the remainder of the twentieth century in an authoritative but readable form. The books in the series, therefore, are of particular interest to parents, governors and all those interested in education, but are written in such a way as to give an overview to student and experienced teachers or other professionals in the field.

Each book gives an account of the relevant legislation and background, but, more importantly, stresses the practical implications of change with specific examples of what is being or can be done to make reforms work effectively. The authors of each book are not only authorities in their field, but also have direct experience of the matters they write about, and that is why the *Education Matters* series makes an important contribution to both debate and practice.

# INTRODUCTION

There are courses about the curriculum at universities. You can get degrees for studying it. And therefore, as with any topic that has taken flight and become a 'subject', there has been a great deal written about it. Moreover, there has also grown a further literature on what one *means* by the curriculum – how it might be defined.

This book aims not at that level of sophistication – or dreariness. It does not say anything very theoretical. And it does not go in for many definitions, believing that definitions begin when real thinking stops. Rather it aims at letting the reader know about and understand some of the immense changes that are taking place in schools as a result of government legislation.

The 1988 Education Reform Act proposed far-reaching changes in how schools and colleges should be organised and in what should be taught within them. One of the results of both this and previous legislation is that more people than before need to know about these changes. Once you could leave all that to the officials in County Hall or to the headteachers who run the schools. If you like, these were professional matters, beyond the understanding and the responsibility of parents or employers or other members of the community.

That, however, is no longer the case. By the end of 1988, there had been a thorough reform of the governing bodies of schools. More parents than ever before are now school governors and there are more representatives of the community, including industry. Moreover, these 'lay people' have more responsibilities than previously – including that of ensuring the National Curriculum is implemented properly.

It is to this group of lay people that this book is directed. It aims to describe in Part One what the position was before the 1988 Education Reform Act – the responsibility for the curriculum, its shape and content and the various forces (such as examinations) which impinged upon it. Part Two shows in what ways the curriculum will have changed because of the Act. As a result of reading the book, it is hoped that the lay person, involved either as parent or as governor in a school, will be better able to participate in school matters, to talk intelligently to the teachers about children's progress, and to ask the right questions of a governing body or parent–teachers association (PTA).

By the curriculum I mean simply the learning experiences that are planned within the school. Often there are happenings, events, which may not be part of an overall plan. I do not want to include these in the curriculum, even if they may be of educational interest. The notion of a plan, of a scheme, of a programme that can be discussed (by governors, say), tried out (by the teachers) and subsequently evaluated, improved or abandoned, is central to the 1988 Education Reform Act – and to this book.

On the other hand, one must never forget that there is a related idea, namely that of the 'hidden curriculum' – what is unsystematically learnt, as a result not of any planned programme, but of the values and relationships and example that exist in the school, often unacknowledged. Nevertheless, the main emphasis of this particular book is firmly on the planned curriculum.

# Part One

# BEFORE THE 1988 EDUCATION REFORM ACT

# Chapter 1

# RESPONSIBILITY FOR THE CURRICULUM

The key legislation in the system of education up to 1988 was the 1944 Education Act. This required the Secretary of State

> to promote the education of the people of England and Wales and the progressive development of institutions devoted to that purpose and to secure the effective execution by local authorities, under his control and direction, of the national policy for providing a varied and comprehensive educational service in every area.

The Act said a lot about the overall framework of the educational service and of how it should be organised. But it said very little about the curriculum. Indeed, apart from religious education, it referred to no subject whatsoever. Rather it allowed the devolution of responsibility for 'delivering education' (and thus the curriculum) to the local education authorities (LEA). Ministers and, later, Secretaries of State had no views on the curriculum, believing it to be a professional matter for teachers.

The LEA owned the schools (except in the cases of those schools that were 'voluntary aided' or 'voluntary controlled'); they paid the teachers even in the 'voluntary schools'; and they made sure that the schools were working efficiently. Even then the responsibility for the quality and content of teaching was, in practice, handed over to the heads and teachers of the respective schools. The curriculum was seen to be a professional matter, and thus to be left in the hands of those who had been trained to develop and to implement it. The governing bodies took little responsibility for the running of the school or for the oversight of the curriculum.

However, in the 1960s there were many indications of how

governments felt this state of affairs to be unsatisfactory. It seemed obvious to some that, if the government were to spend so much on education (indirectly through the rate support grant to LEAs), then it should monitor more carefully and influence what was taught in schools. Moreover, there were growing concerns among employers, parents, politicians and others about the content, relevance and standards of the school curriculum. Many of these misgivings may have been misplaced, but misgivings there were. Roughly speaking these criticisms were of four kinds.

First, the school curriculum was not equipping young people adequately for the world of work. Employers were saying that the people who came to them at 16 or 18 (or, indeed, in their early twenties straight from university or polytechnics) had not the basic skills or the appropriate personal qualities or the right attitudes. Something simply had to be done to rectify that.

Secondly, ever since the publication by right-wing thinkers of the Black Papers in the 1960s, schools had been criticised for shoddy standards. Standards were slipping, so it was said. And subsequently there has been much debate over whether that is so. It is not an easy debate to resolve. Facts and figures are bandied about. The increased number of people passing examinations is quoted on one side of the argument, but the significance of these figures is disputed on the other. Praise and blame (depending on where you stand) are attributed to child-centred approaches to the curriculum.

Thirdly, it is felt that young people are being inadequately prepared for the future, not only economically (i.e. with the skills industry needs) but psychologically or personally. They are facing a difficult and unpredictable future. And they need the personal and moral qualities to face life when it gets tough.

Finally, the increasing violence and vandalism in society at large is sometimes attributed to schools – the lack of discipline or, once again, the so-called child-centred methods. There needs, according to this criticism, to be a much greater emphasis on citizenship and on the extended curriculum activities which foster discipline and a sense of responsibility.

These, then, are background criticisms against which we must view the government's various attempts to reform the curriculum. Readers will no doubt feel able to associate with some of these complaints; with some others, they may ask 'Where is the evidence?' The remainder, they may wish to reject as unsubstantiated or untrue. The truth or otherwise does not matter too much for my purpose, which is essentially that of giving the background to, and thereby explaining, present changes in the curriculum.

However, I need to point out, in anticipation of what is to come, the real difficulties that schools have in meeting so many different sorts of criticism. After all, 'improvement in standards' is often interpreted as the need to concentrate on the traditional subjects and methods, which, however, have failed and alienated so many children – thus giving rise to personal frustration and to the rejection of educational values. Or, again, the entrenchment of traditional values may leave little place for a more obvious preparation for the future – after all, links with industry or economic awareness or work experience did not have a place in the grammar school curriculum we knew a generation ago.

None the less, in the light of these criticisms, there was launched, after a keynote speech by Prime Minister James Callaghan in 1976, what came to be called the 'great debate' when ministers and civil servants went around the country holding public debates on the curriculum. Following that, the government asked LEAs to furnish details of their respective curriculum policies and initiated a series of consultation and policy papers on the curriculum. The curriculum was no longer the private concern of a profession, but a matter of public interest and importance.

This chapter gives a very brief history of these documents – the increasing focus upon balance between subjects and the ever more detailed account of what those subjects should contain. That is important. The 1988 legislation did not come out of the blue. It is a stage in a process whereby the government has come to interpret its responsibilities under the 1944 Education Act (namely 'to promote the education of the people of England and Wales') in a more direct and centralised way. Immediately, however, I am concerned with delineating the responsibility for the curriculum.

## Governing bodies

In many respects, the governing bodies had been fairly ineffective in the running of the schools. The curriculum was a matter for the head. The maintenance of the school, the appointment and the payment of teachers, the admissions policy, the relations between schools, etc., were largely a matter for the LEA. But there were voices that said that the balance of the partnership (between government, LEAs and teachers) that controlled education needed to change. Where were parents in the partnership? Where were employers and other members of the community?

In 1977, the Taylor Committee produced its report 'A New Partnership for our Schools'. The Committee argued that the governing bodies should exercise the power and perform the functions as these were outlined in the 1944 Education Act but largely ignored. The Committee made several recommendations. First, it recommended equal representation on the governing bodies of parents, teachers, LEAs and the community. Secondly, the governing bodies should, within the overall policy of the LEA, determine the general direction of school policy, including that for the curriculum. Indeed, there was

> no area of the schools' activities in respect of which the governing body should have no responsibility, nor on which the head and the staff should be accountable only to themselves or to the local education authority.

Subsequent legislation has put into effect many of the ideas in the Taylor Report. The 1980 Education Act changed the

Instruments of Government such that teachers and parents must have a place on the governing bodies; and it obliged the governors to publish the sort of information about the school and its curriculum that would help parents make informed choices. Furthermore, the governors were increasingly asked to study, and to have a view upon, the many curriculum papers that the Department of Education and Science (DES) was distributing. Gradually, the governing bodies were being initiated into their responsibilities for the school curriculum.

The 1986 Education Act went further. It increased the number of parent and community representatives on the governing bodies. And it extended their powers and responsibilities – in anticipation of the 1988 Education Reform Act which devolved to governing bodies responsibility for approximately 75 per cent of the total cost of running a school if it has over 200 pupils, and above all responsibility for making sure that the curriculum of the school reflects the requirements of the various Education Acts. And that means conformity to the detailed programmes of study to be established under the National Curriculum. But the 1986 Act also included responsibility for establishing a policy on sex education and for ensuring that political indoctrination does not take place.

Therefore, we can see a shift in the partnership that provides education from 5 to 16: greater parental and community presence and thus the involvement of non-professionals in the deliberations over educational values and over the content of the curriculum. The role of the LEA is thereby diminished and the monopoly over curriculum removed from the teachers.

What then do governors do?

1. They are responsible for the general conduct of the school, and advise the head on such matters as discipline policy.
2. They must make sure that the curriculum meets the requirements of the National Curriculum.
3. They must check that full and proper information is given

to parents concerning the curriculum and examinations.
4. They keep an eye on the way in which the school handles controversial issues – particularly those of sex and political education.

But although this signifies an increase in local power and responsibility, with the 'consumer' (parent and employer) now having a view on the curriculum that must be heard, local power and responsibility must be exercised within the tighter and more detailed framework that has been emerging from the government.

## Local education authorities (LEAs)

One of the three elements in the partnership that was responsible for the provision of education was the LEA, of which there are about 100 in England and Wales. The LEAs employ the teachers and own the schools, except in the cases of voluntary-aided and voluntary-controlled schools. The LEAs provide, from rates and the government's Rate Support Grant, the money for building, maintaining and running the schools. And the LEAs have responsibility for ensuring there is a properly run school with a curriculum that meets the needs of the children. To carry out this policy, the LEAs employ advisers or inspectors, career officers and a team of psychologists.

Until the early 1980s, most LEAs would have had little or no detailed knowledge of the curriculum under their care since this was seen as the business of the professionals in the school. But several things have happened to change all that. First, the government requires of LEAs information about the curriculum of their schools; it requires reassurance that its policies, as they are developed in documents I refer to below, are being implemented; above all, it is increasingly making funding conditional upon the LEAs shaping the curriculum in a particular way. For instance, a lot of money was made available to make the curriculum more technical and vocational – but only if the LEAs (and thus the schools) met certain

9

conditions laid down by the Manpower Services Commission (MSC), now the Training Agency.

Furthermore, the LEA's power lay partly in being able to raise the money (through the rates) to shape the school system as it thought fit. But this has become more and more difficult in recent years, as the government finds various ways to restrict public expenditure. Local authorities are no longer able to raise rates to find the money to do what they want – to do over and above what is required in order to meet the wishes of government.

In many respects, therefore, the LEA's power was diminishing before the 1988 Education Reform Act – conceding its place in the partnership to central government. Instead, the LEA, particularly through its inspectorate, has been moving towards the more executive functions of:

- seeking resources from central government
- distributing them to schools in accordance with national priorities
- monitoring performance within schools
- advising schools on curriculum matters
- ensuring adequate numbers of teachers and buildings for the curriculum to be implemented to all who want to go to the LEA schools.

None the less, in doing all these things, the LEAs were obliged, under the 1986 Education Act, to have a policy on the curriculum that would be implemented in schools and that would comply with the emerging national framework.

**Teachers**

The ultimate responsibility for the curriculum is the governors', within the framework agreed by the LEA. Usually that responsibility has been devolved to the headteacher, who will share it (in different degrees) with the teachers themselves. The degree of sharing will depend on the size of the school and the managerial style of the head. Of course, the larger the school, the less able is the headteacher to have control over all aspects of the curriculum. And, indeed, why should he or she? Teachers are professionals. They have been trained academically and through experience to design and to implement the curriculum of their class or of their subject. No headteacher, surely, should tell a qualified mathematics teacher what and how to teach. Teachers, moreover, may belong to subject associations or to other professional groups. As a *historian*, the secondary-school teacher will make judgements over what to teach in history and how to teach it. As a trained *primary* specialist, the teacher of 8- or 9-year-olds will decide what they should be taught in environmental studies, say, or in mathematics.

At least, that is how it was until recently. But there are three major reasons why this level of responsibility has been first, challenged and, subsequently, diminished.

First, as we see in the aims of the curriculum listed later (see page 23) and reiterated in several DES and HMI (Her Majesty's Inspectorate of Schools) documents, what you teach depends very much on what you value, and teachers are no more experts on values than are parents, employers and other members of the community. Many parents feel that they also have a say in what should be taught because they have ideas about the sort of person they would like their children to grow up to be. Moreover, they are at the receiving-end of children who come home frustrated and 'failed' by the curriculum. Hence, there is a need for more participation by people other than teachers in deciding what the educational aims should be.

Secondly, increasingly there is seen to be a need for a shared framework, such as that suggested by the DES and by HMI in the various documents I shall summarise. This will ensure continuity and progression. Otherwise one teacher might not build upon what was taught by the last teacher of the children under his or her care.

Thirdly, the government feels it necessary to direct the curriculum in a particular way to meet national and economic interests, which may not be appreciated by all teachers.

Fourthly, there are incompetent teachers – just as there are incompetent lawyers, doctors and accountants. And it is thought that more prescription of what should be taught will alleviate this problem.

Teachers' responsibility and control – their professional status – does, therefore, seem to be diminished. Perhaps teachers had too much power. Perhaps there should be a more significant place for parents especially – through their representatives on the newly constituted governing bodies. But there are dangers unless one is careful. Too much undermining of the professional role of teachers might drive the best ones away and make recruitment difficult. It might encourage a certain mindless and mechanical approach to planning the curriculum. After all, unless the teachers are convinced of the educational sense of what they are expected to do, no amount of government planning will have any effect. It is the teacher not the Civil Servant who, day after day, is in the classroom.

## External examinations

In Chapter 4 I look in greater detail at arrangements for examining and assessing. But in this preliminary account of the responsibility for the curriculum prior to the 1988 Education Reform Act, one cannot ignore the role of examination boards. After all, they set the objectives which, if ignored, will mean that the students come out of school as failures, unable perhaps to progress to the kind of training or employment that they want to follow.

Once upon a time, nearly all primary school children would have taken the 11+ Examination (the scholarship). On the basis of the results, a minority would have been selected for grammar schools, the remainder on the whole going to secondary modern schools. That examination, based mainly on verbal reasoning, intelligence and mathematical tests, influenced (and most would say 'narrowed') the curriculum. Teachers felt obliged to teach to the test. The abolition of the 11+ in most places freed teachers to broaden the curriculum and not to have to teach 'to a test'.

Secondary schools, however, do remain very much constrained by examination. Many would say that this is a good thing. Examinations are the most effective way of influencing the curriculum. They establish the objectives – what is to be learnt.

The main examination to know about is, of course, the General Certificate of Secondary Education (GCSE). From autumn 1986, this replaced the two quite different examinations, GCE and CSE. Grades are awarded on a scale A to G, with moderation provided by one of the regional examination boards (for example, the Southern Examining Board). GCSEs are subject-specific. That is, GCSE provides different and discrete examinations for different subjects that are approved by the Secretary of State. It does not *explicitly* examine those qualities and skills that cross subject boundaries. But it was the government's intention that the new examinations would require a greater emphasis upon experiential learning (that is, upon the kinds of experience that the pupils bring into the school and that may not be related to any particular subject) and upon practical work, on process and on problem-solving skills, even if that meant that less content was covered. Possibly this has had more impact upon teaching than anything else.

Eventually, each grade in each subject will represent a set of criteria which set out what successful candidates can do. Hence, the examinations will be 'criterion-referenced', rather than norm-referenced as was the case with GCE. The difference might be illustrated as follows. A number of people could be taking a driving test. If it was decided that only a certain percentage should be allowed to pass, then it would be important to put the applicants in some rank-order of poorest to the best. Only the top percentage would then be allowed to pass, no matter how much those below the established norm for passing know or can do. That would be the norm-referenced approach to testing. Another approach, however, would be that of allowing all to pass who meet certain criteria of successful performance which have been established beforehand. Thus it would be no use a candidate claiming he had got 90 per cent

13

of the driving test right and should pass, even though he flattened a 'Keep Left' sign. On a criterion-referenced test, you either meet the criteria or you do not. In making GCSE more and more criterion-referenced, the examination boards need to spell out much more clearly what students must be able to do to achieve the different grades.

Each subject is divided into at least three 'domains'. For example, English is divided into oral communication, reading, and writing; geography into specific geographical knowledge, geographical understanding, map and graphic skills, and application of geography to economic, environmental, political and social issues. Within each domain, levels of performance are specified and candidates achieve points for demonstrations of competence. The points scored in each domain are aggregated to produce the final grade (A to G).

Although there is general agreement in the value of this examination reform, criticisms have been made. One is that the shift to much more practical and course work has made life almost impossible for teacher and pupil alike – but that, no doubt, is a matter of balance that can be adjusted over time. None the less, parents will have experienced much more activity, searching for resources, investigations, etc. The curriculum, determined by examinations, is fostering a different style of learning.

Another criticism is that it is difficult to ensure the differentiation of treatment between pupils, advocated by the DES and HMI (see page 28) within a single examination structure. And either (as in French or mathematics) you put students in for different examination papers within the same structure or you try to organise the course work or the examination questions so that students can respond at different levels of sophistication.

It is important to remember, however, that in the case of each examination under each examination board, the criteria for the grades have to conform to national criteria and to be agreed by the Secretary of State. In this way, there is another form of central control.

There are examinations other than the GCSE that can be taken at 16+ and which enable other kinds of things to be achieved through the curriculum. The Business and Technician Education Council (BTEC) and the City and Guilds of London Institute (CGLI) do jointly offer a pre-vocational Foundation Programme which is designed to make learning more 'relevant', helping to bridge the gap between school and subsequent training or employment. These Foundation Programmes are designed around a series of 'case studies' which provide:

- activity-based learning opportunities – such as running a small business;
- opportunities for acquiring useful skills;
- a profiling of what the young person can do which will help determine what should be learnt and also present a positive picture to employer or teacher;
- a vehicle for guidance and counselling;
- a more integrated educational experience.

This new development, which is proving popular with schools, can be taken side by side with GCSE, but it does represent a very different curriculum policy. And about this I shall have more to say in Chapters 2 and 4.

## Government

The government did, until comparatively recently, have little to say about the curriculum. But in the 1960s and particularly the 1970s, it came to influence and finally prescribe in a much more direct manner. There are three kinds of documents through which this has happened. They relate to the curriculum and are increasingly examined as a matter of course by governing bodies.

### Committee reports

When the government, as a result very often of dissatisfactions expressed by advisers or politicians or employers or teachers, sees that there is a need for a thorough review of some area of the curriculum, it will set up a committee to look into it and to report back. Very often these reports result not in further legislation but in a much better understanding of the problems as a basis for further curriculum development and training of teachers. Therefore, in coming to understand the present-day curriculum and to identify the important questions to ask, it is often a good idea to start with these reports.

**Bullock Report: A Language for Life (1975)**

It is always arbitrary to start one's account at a particular date. Why not the Plowden Report on primary education in 1967, or the Newsom Report on (the lower) half of our future in 1958, or indeed the Spens Report on Secondary Education in 1938?

There have, however, been some important shifts in curriculum thinking in the last decade or so, and there have been reports that still dominate that thinking – reference points in the debate. A major one is the Bullock Report, and so there we start.

Many parents of primary-school children will expect to see a fairly systematic and disciplined approach to the teaching of reading and writing – graded readers, the well-ordered build-up of words, the simplification of words into their phonic parts (i.e. into their more basic sounds), the rote learning of spellings, etc. And in secondary schools there will be expectations that clearly marked on the timetable will be English language, in which these early lessons are continued – spelling, writing skills, grammar, reading, and so on. Indeed, such expectations will be reinforced by the frequent criticisms of schools, especially from employers, that standards are not what they used to be, and that we are producing too many future employees without the required standards of literacy (i.e. who cannot read or write).

It was in response to such criticisms that the government established a committee 'to enquire into the teaching in the schools of reading and the other uses of English'. The final report was a thorough survey of the practice and the theory of English teaching and quickly became a textbook in the training of teachers and in the staff development of teachers. Its main points were:

- there simply is no evidence to show the widespread deterioration of literacy, but the different demands that society now made upon young people required a higher standard all round;
- we could not be satisfied that what was achieved in schools met these different demands;
- there must be a much broader and more generous picture of what achievement in English consisted in: talking and listening as well as reading and writing;
- talking, listening, reading, and writing had different *functions* in different *contexts* as one addressed different *audiences*;
- and, therefore, the drills and exercises that often take place outside any realistic context but that many parents want to see, were quite inappropriate for the development of language skills needed to meet different functions with different audiences in mind;
- since language, understood in the broader sense, was basic to all that we do (to science, to relationships, to decision-making), then the responsibility for the teaching of English (for improving the skills of talking, listening, reading and writing) belonged to *all* teachers.

According to the Bullock Report, therefore, there must be a language policy *across the curriculum*.

The significance of the Bullock Report for the development of our curriculum thinking cannot be overestimated. First, we cannot see the curriculum to be split up into discrete and unrelated subjects. Language skills lie at the base of learning in all the subjects, and therefore language development must be given pre-eminence. Secondly, we must get into the habit of cross-curriculum thinking and planning. A parent should be able to receive from the school its *language* policy affecting *all* subjects and activities.

## Warnock Report: Special Educational Needs (1978)

The Warnock Report is important not simply because of what it says (although it is the first report ever to provide a comprehensive picture of the education of the handicapped), but because of what happened as a result of it.

First, then, let us look at what it says about matters closely related to the concern of this book. It argues that many more young people have special educational needs – so many, in fact, that you cannot really talk about overall curriculum planning as though most children are 'normal', that is without difficulties that make it necessary to adjust the curriculum to learning difficulties. In fact, it argues that 20 per cent of pupils have special educational needs at some stage of their schooling – 'special' in the sense of warranting special provision and help. The Report, in so stretching the concept of 'special need', recommended an abolition of different categories of handicap and the integration, as much as possible, of children with special needs into the mainstream of education. But, of course, that has implications for the curriculum and for the style of teaching within mainstream education. One 'hidden' advantage might be the increased sensitivity and awareness of children, within mainstream education, to the problems that handicap other children – hardly a timetabled curriculum subject, but part of the curriculum in a broader, life-enhancing sense!

Secondly, an effort has been made to integrate young people as much as possible into ordinary schools and to bring in the specialist curriculum help that such an integration requires. A child who cannot cope with the curriculum might receive specialist diagnostic or medical help and, if a statement is given to the effect that special help is required within the school, then the LEA is obliged to provide it. The main point for our purposes, however, is that any school has to look at its curriculum with special needs in mind – the provision that needs to be made for different forms of handicap and for various forms of remedial solution to poor learning.

## Cockcroft Report: Mathematics Counts (1982)

This report was in many respects similar in origin and in importance to the Bullock Report. There was public concern over standards in mathematics – too many pupils seemed to be learning too little. Reasons for this concern seemed to lie in poorly qualified teachers (many were not qualified in that subject) and, so it was felt, in the lack of agreement over objectives at different ages. The Report did recommend a foundation list of mathematical topics for the bottom 40 per cent of the ability range in secondary schools which would involve a much more practical and relevant approach. The curriculum should differentiate between pupils much more, recognising the different levels of ability and the different purposes mathematics might serve. In spelling this out more clearly, the Report looked closely at the mathematical needs of adult life – at home as well as in employment. As a result, it stated that all children in preparation for adult life should have the ability to read numbers and to count, to tell the time, to pay for purchases and to give change, to weigh and to measure, to understand straightforward timetables and simple graphs and charts and to carry out any necessary calculations associated with these, and to make approximate estimates in lengths, areas, capacities and weights. Above all, it tackled the problem of lack of confidence that many, even able, people feel in their mathematical ability. It also addressed the problem of the relatively poor performance of girls. Although the Report did not endorse much of the 'back to basics' lobby (rote learning of tables, concentration on the skills of adding, subtracting, multiplying and dividing), it did recommend a greater emphasis upon mental and oral work ('doing it in your head').

## The Swann Report: Education for All (1985)

This is the fourth of the background reports of a government committee of enquiry that I want to draw readers' attention to. The Report was concerned with the kind of education that *all* should receive as a preparation for life in a society which is both multiracial and culturally diverse. Hence, it had two main focuses: how might the education of the white majority be affected and how might that of the minority from the other ethnic groups? Obviously, it is mainly a curriculum problem: do we need to inject a different or an added content, do we simply have to examine our teaching styles, or do we have to give particular attention to the needs of distinguishable groups? In seeking answers to these questions, the Report commences with a chapter on 'the nature of society' – to get the curriculum right you must take into account the social context in which you are teaching. What it concludes is that in a pluralist society, differences need to be understood and respected. Therefore, the Report argues for a 'multicultural approach', especially in (but by no means confined to) religious education.

### The Kingman Report: The Teaching of English Language (1988)

This recommended a model of English language which could be used for determining what should be taught at school and what knowledge, therefore, the teachers should have in order to teach effectively. In anticipation of the National Curriculum, it does set out attainment targets for 7, 11 and 16-year-olds. In this, the Report's importance lies in the responses it embodies to the criticisms about falling standards. Some of those criticisms suggest that there should be a return to 'traditional methods' of language teaching – lots of exercises, drilling, rote learning, spelling tests: that sort of thing. The Report, however, is clearly against 'old fashioned grammar teaching and learning by rote'. On the other hand, it expressed concern about certain views that are current in some schools, namely, that one should not prescribe a standard form of English. The Report argues that 'Equally at the other extreme, we reject the belief that any notion of correct or incorrect use of language is an affront to personal liberty. We also reject the belief that knowing how to use terminology in which to speak of language (e.g. "nouns", "adjectives", "tenses") is undesirable.'

The model of language put forward is fourfold:

1. *The forms of the English language*: sounds, letters, words, sentences, and how these relate to meaning.
2. *Communication and comprehension*: how speakers and writers communicate and how listeners and readers understand them.
3. *Acquisition and development*: how the child acquires and develops language.
4. *Historical and geographical variation*: how language changes over time, and how languages which are spread over territories differentiate into dialects or indeed into separate languages.

This is more a model for teacher training than for teaching pupils, but it is based upon a view of what children should know and be able to do. Therefore, the Report sets out fourteen attainment targets for 16-year-olds, fifteen for 11-year-olds, and fourteen for 7-year-olds. Some of these targets are what children should know explicitly or consciously – for example, the differences between verbs and adverbs. Others are implicit knowledge – knowing *how* to write coherently and intelligently without necessarily knowing explicitly the rules that one needs to obey in order to be coherent and intelligible. The Kingman Report was a forerunner of the Cox Reports on primary and secondary English teaching, which were published in 1988 and 1989 as part of the National Curriculum planning exercise.

These, then, are five major reports from government commissions of enquiry. They set out important curriculum principles and specific recommendations. These would include: the importance of thinking across the curriculum, and not simply in separate subjects; the need to be more practical in the kind of knowledge and skill to be fostered; the value of setting out more clearly a shared framework within which the curriculum might be seen to develop from 5 to 16; and more attention to be given to differences between children whether those differences arise out of ethnic origin or ability.

## Government consultation papers

The government sets up committees of enquiry, such as those I have referred to above, which provide thorough surveys of the background to a problem (standards of English teaching or of mathematical ability, or educational policy with special-needs children or with minorities). The reports of such enquiries serve several purposes. They become, for example, the basis of the staff development of teachers. But they can also become the basis of government policy, even legislation.

The government – in order to clarify its own views, or to set the agenda for a national debate, or to prepare the way for subsequent legislation – will publish consultation documents. The increasing number of these in recent years reflects the growing encroachment of government on the curriculum that once was seen to be the privileged area of teachers.

In 'A Framework for the School Curriculum' (1980), the government produced (as a result of the 'great debate' on education inaugurated three years earlier by the then Secretary of State, Shirley Williams) a barely disguised prescription for the kind of curriculum that the DES would like to see. It was spelt out mainly in terms of subjects, and recommended percentages of the entire timetable for special subject areas, core subjects: English, maths, science, foreign language, religious education (RE) and physical education (PE). Options would supplement the core compulsory subjects, thus providing choice between subjects. At the same time, non-subject considerations were emphasised: moral education, preparation for parenthood and for employment, careers guidance, work experience, and personal and social education. Craft, design and technology (CDT) also, it should be mentioned, got a robust welcome.

Hence 'A Framework for the School Curriculum' was already reflecting a shift in government thinking away from the role of sleeping partner to that of adviser, strongly suggesting a particular shape and content of the curriculum. Needless to say, the professional reaction was loud, long, and rather scornful.

'The School Curriculum' (1981), only one year later, re-emphasised the aims of 'A Framework'. The aims were:

- to help pupils to develop lively, enquiring minds, the ability to question and argue rationally and to apply themselves to tasks, and physical skills;
- to help pupils to acquire knowledge and skills relevant to adult life and employment in a fast-changing world;
- to help pupils to use language and numbers effectively;
- to instil respect for religious and moral values, and tolerance of other races, religions and ways of life;
- to help pupils to understand the world in which they live, and the interdependence of individuals, groups and nations;
- to help pupils to appreciate human achievements and aspirations.

'The School Curriculum' then went on to spell out the way in which the curriculum might do this by repeating essentially the same list of subjects as 'A Framework' but, this time, omitting the percentage of time desirably spent on each subject.

The question we do need to ask, however, is how might these general aims relate to subjects as they are generally understood and taught. The first aim would seem to require a more open, stimulating approach to teaching: a concern for relating what is learnt to life beyond school, and a moral dimension to learning, rather than any specific subject matter.

'Better Schools' (1985) was a government White Paper that pulled together much of the work and enquiries conducted by both the DES and HMI over the previous few years, and, in the light of it all, enunciated general curriculum principles – as well as recommendations on the organisation and management of schools and LEAs. It started, as had other reports, with an expression of concern over the quality of school education, and with the reassertion of the government's aims to raise standards and to provide the skills and knowledge required for national prosperity. To achieve those aims, there has to be:

- Better curriculum planning and management, with clearer learning objectives, than is usually to be found;
- A broader experience than concentration upon the basics;
- More oral and practical work;
- Greater differentiation between pupils in teacher setting of work;
- Less dependence on teacher-directed learning;
- A closer relationship between curriculum objectives and the way in which students' work is assessed and recorded.

The White Paper is best known for its emphasis upon four principles that should characterise the curriculum:

1. *Broad*: introduction to a wide range of areas of experience, knowledge and skill (see, for example, the areas of experience outlined by HMI on page 27, and above by 'A Framework for the School Curriculum' and by 'The School Curriculum');
2. *Balanced*: the careful allocation of time between these different areas;
3. *Relevant*: the linking of what is taught both to the pupil's own experience and to the next stage of the person's life, especially adult life and the world of employment (for which reason there needs to be much more practical work in schools and a greater stress upon technology);
4. *Differentiated*: clearly related to the distinctive abilities and needs of different children (and in this reference is made to the Cockcroft Report – see page 19).

'Records of Achievement: A Statement of Policy' (1984) was a very different kind of document, but most important in our understanding of curriculum developments. Both teachers and employers are very often dissatisfied with traditional examinations, though for different reasons. Examinations do give information about only one small part of what some students have achieved during the period of their schooling. Moreover, even this information is inadequate. It says what grade a student has received in mathematics, say, but it does not convey any information about what he or she can do or say or know. Way back in 1958, the Newsom Report, 'Half our Future', said that 'boys and girls who stay at school until they are 16 may reasonably look for some record of achievement when they leave', which will give this much more generous profile of achievement to all young people. The 1984 statement establishes this as government policy to be in operation by 1990.

The purpose of such a record of achievement is fourfold:

1. To recognise achievement in more than just public examinations;
2. To contribute to pupils' personal development and progress by improving their motivation and increasing their awareness of strengths and weaknesses;
3. To help schools identify the all-round potential of their pupils;
4. To provide young people leaving school with a short summary document which is recognised and valued by employers and institutions of further and higher education.

Records of achievement are a significant part now of the developing curriculum. They are a response to criticism both of employers in terms of relevance of school to the world of work and of parents and teachers in terms of the personal needs that school must serve. But the implementation of this policy will make demands upon the timetable and upon the energy and time of the teachers which have not been fully recognised.

These, then, are just four of the several government consultation papers that preceded the National Curriculum and that both anticipated what was to come and spelt out the rather mixed attempts to meet the criticisms that I briefly referred to on page 5. At the same time, there has been a series of White Papers jointly from the Department of Employment and the DES, which propose much closer links between education and vocational training. In particular, 'Education and Training for Young People' (1985) outlined the government's policy to provide work-related courses between the ages of 14 and

18 in full-time education, mainly through vocational-oriented courses (see page 50 about TVEI), and links between school and industry (see page 102). And, therefore, in these documents we see several different strands of thinking with different recommendations. First, there is an insistence upon the traditional organisation of learning in recognised subjects. Secondly, there is the importance attached to personal development which cannot be confined to work within these subjects. And thirdly there is the stress upon links between school and industry – which is neither traditional nor necessarily person-centred. But it could be, if those responsible for the curriculum get it right.

### Her Majesty's Inspectorate (HMI)

It is not correct to see government influence in the curriculum exercised through HMI. HMI rightly values and jealously guards its professional independence – hence, *Her Majesty's* Inspectorate, not the government's. HMI was 'created' over 100 years ago and its job is to inspect schools, to check and monitor standards of teaching within those schools, to advise schools and LEAs on curriculum and other matters, and to advise, too, the government on the professional aspect of its educational responsibilities. In that last respect, HMI has been called the 'ears and eyes' of government. Inspectors are scattered throughout the UK and thus, collectively, are aware of any significant developments or problems in the schools of each locality. At the same time, due to this knowledge and also to their own expertise, they are able to advise government on policy, which advice the Secretary of State may or may not accept. There are several documents (or sets of documents) that HMI have produced with this intention, including the following.

### 'Curriculum 11–16' (1977)

This was a consultation paper that aimed to develop an agreed framework for the curriculum at secondary level. The document provided the analytic thinking that was a prerequisite for curriculum planning. The analytic framework consisted of areas of experience in which development should take place, mainly, though not exclusively, through the agency of subjects. These areas of experience were:

- aesthetic and creative
- ethical
- linguistic
- mathematical
- scientific
- physical
- social and political
- spiritual

The appendices to the report contained detailed check-lists of objectives within each of the areas. These objectives related to a wide range of subjects which by no means fitted directly into the respective areas. The difference between HMI thinking in this document and DES thinking in 'School Curriculum' (see page 23) is important. The DES thought in terms of subjects; HMI in terms of areas of experience which transcended subject boundaries.

### 'Primary Education in England' (1978)

HMI used a similar analytic approach in this survey, though with a slightly different formula, namely:

- language and literacy
- mathematics
- science
- aesthetics, including PE
- social abilities, including RE

Even in a totally integrated curriculum, one needs to distinguish distinctive areas where development is to be encouraged.

### 'A View of the Curriculum' (1980)

This summarised HMI thinking as a result of these, the survey of secondary schools, and the vast HMI experience of schools. It spelt out the main problem that any curriculum has to face – namely, providing a general education for everybody while respecting and catering for individual differences. Too often we forget the special needs of children – whether those who are particularly able or those who, through learning blockages or disabilities, find learning difficult. The importance of *differentiation* is a key element in this 'view of the curriculum'. On the other hand, commonality can be ensured if, whatever the differences, the curriculum contributes to the same 'areas of experience' that are described above. The *principles* of curriculum development, therefore, are: breadth, differentiation, continuity – and agreement on essential areas of knowledge, understanding and skills.

However, the most significant contribution to the current debate by HMI has been its 'Curriculum Matters' series. In this, it has, for major subjects like English, science, mathematics and others, spelt out the aims, framework, principles and content of curriculum design from 5 to 16. This model is given on pages 30–58.

### Conclusion

To understand the importance of the 1988 Education Reform Act, you have to understand, too, the situation and the opinions that gave rise to it. The immediate period of consultation was very short indeed – almost a travesty of consultation. But, in many respects, both the curriculum content embodied within the Act and the changed responsibility for the curriculum had been anticipated in a series of reports, consultation documents, examination changes and centralising decisions over ten years or more.

Education, it was felt, was not coming up to standard: it was not meeting the needs of society, especially industry, and it was not enabling young people to get the best out of life. What was needed, it was felt, was an agreed curriculum framework with a greater degree of prescription, and this could be achieved through more government direction. How this took place I shall explain in Chapters 3, 4 and 5.

# Chapter 2

# THE CURRICULUM 5 TO 16

According to the 1944 Education Act, schools need to be divided into primary and secondary. The break is usually at the age of 11, but, especially as a result of the reorganisation into a comprehensive system, the change-over date is sometimes 12, sometimes indeed 13. Furthermore, some secondary schools take students up to 18, others only up to 16 – the 16-year-olds then moving on to tertiary colleges, to colleges of further education or to sixth form colleges. This generally confusing state of affairs can best be illustrated by reference to the different patterns of education all within a 20-mile radius of my home-town of Exeter (Figure 2.1).

This rather messy organisation of education is exacerbated by the possibility of transfer across the systems within such a small geographical area – at 11, say, from the 8 to 12 middle-school system into the 11 to 18 secondary system, or at 16 from the 11 to 18 secondary system into the 16 to 18 tertiary system.

This variety of systems, with the possibility of mobility between them, demonstrates how important is the question of development and continuity in the curriculum – planning from 5 to 16 across a range of institutions. It is partly in answer to this problem that the government has proposed a National Curriculum from 5 to 16.

This book is concerned with the curriculum during these compulsory years of schooling. However, for some, school begins in nursery school; for many, it continues into the sixth form or the further-education sector; and therefore the National Curriculum should ensure continuity between these two 'end-on' phases.

'Primary' normally refers to the period 5 to 11, but, where

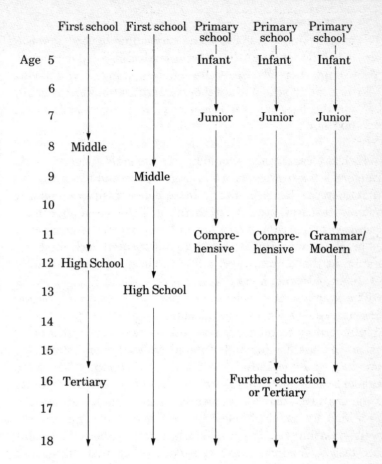

**Figure 2.1**

there is a middle-school phase of 8 to 12, it includes 12-year-olds as well. This phase is itself normally divided into two – the infant stage and the junior (or, as in Exeter, into First and Middle Schools). Sometimes each stage takes place in a quite separate school with its own headteacher and governing body. More often, the two stages are combined. Whatever the organisation, continuity from 5 to 11 or 12 must be an important curriculum issue.

31

## The infant stage

The content and the shape of the curriculum depend so much on the philosophy and the educational aims of the teacher. You would, therefore, see quite different things if you moved from one infant school to another. Generalisations are difficult.

None the less, there is some measure of agreement about five matters.

1. These early years should enable the child to have a wide range of *sensory experience* – seeing, feeling and listening – so that they can learn to discriminate between shapes, colours, sounds, textures, etc. The importance of this often goes unrecognised by parents, who want to know about the purpose of so much activity. But it should be argued that such discrimination at the sensory level forms the basis of understanding at a more abstract level.

For example, the various activities in which young people discriminate between kinds of objects (beads, perhaps), possibly according to colour or size, are basic to the logical operations of classification and of the identification of instances of class which are essential to mathematical thinking. The same can be said of 'matching' – linking sets of objects according to some feature, such as texture or shape. Often parents are mystified by so much pleasant but apparently purposeless activity. What they expect and want is more paperwork – sums and tables. The infant teacher needs to show that subsequent mathematical development will depend not so much on early memory work ('learning off the tables') but on that 'feeling for' and imaginary understanding of what you *do* when you count, subtract or multiply.

The same argument can be applied to early scientific development. Basic to science is a sense of curiosity, a wanting to know why things happen or what makes things work. I recently listened to a talk by a well-known scientist with an international reputation, who told an audience of young people that the spirit that created the good scientist, engineer and technologist was the insatiable curiosity which made them want to take things apart and to see the inner workings. This spirit of enquiry – awkward though it can be for parents who do not like to see their television or telephone in bits and pieces – is one which needs to be encouraged early. There is no point in the abstractions of science (often absorbed through rote learning as one sits at a desk) without the *practical* grasp of the ideas and concepts gained through *doing* science. And the most important job at this early age is to instil this spirit of enquiry and to do so with a view to making children realise that all events have causes and that there is an explanation for whatever happens. Very general concepts of cause and effect are thus implicitly introduced.

2. The early years are vitally important in developing *personal and social skills*. Even at the age of 5, the differences between children can be quite dramatic in such things as: how to play with other children and share things, how to control feelings and emotions, how to talk or listen to adults including the teacher, or how to face and to take responsibility for everyday practical problems. Therefore, the good infant teacher will concentrate a lot of energy upon the gradual development of co-operation, sharing, independence in practical matters, and self-confidence. And this can be achieved only if the infants are given practical and social tasks to do. These can be: the distribution of paper, pencils and other resources; separate contributions to a wall-painting for Christmas; the sharing of resources in mathematics; looking after the fish or the classroom gerbil; taking care of a new member of the class. Of course, the development of such personal and social qualities does not have specific time devoted to it. It is not a separate subject. Rather it is a way of approaching teaching and of relating to young people. By having such personal and social development foremost in their minds, the infant teachers simply organise their teaching differently and they constantly look out for opportunities to encourage co-operation, a sense of achievement, sharing, group work and so on.

3. The early years are essential to the subsequent development of *language skills* – not simply reading and writing, but

talking and listening, too. Once again, parents often want to see much more book work, corrected spellings: *evidence* that their child has done something (and there is no doubting the fact that some private preparatory schools sell themselves to over-anxious parents by advertising such 'traditional methods' or 'traditional standards'). But good writing requires a command of language, and a facility with it, which depends upon exposure (from a very early age) to the richness of language and to a lot of oral experience. That richness is of two kinds. First, there is a richness of experience about which one is encouraged to talk, seeking to communicate that experience to others. It is foolish to try to improve children's ability to write or to talk, unless they have something to write about – and the liveliness of mind to make them want to write about it. And the alert teacher will always be creating situations (or capitalising on those that occur in the normal course of school life) that will enrich and stimulate the children's imaginations – actively, positively, providing the urge to express and to communicate that which is experienced. Secondly, however, there is a richness of the vocabulary and the modes of expression through which the children record and communicate that experience. Once again, the alert teacher will constantly be extending the vocabulary of the infants, helping them to make distinctions, to be precise, to find the right word, to explain what is seen. Without language one can hardly think, and without talking and listening and trying to communicate, one will be very limited in one's capacity to write.

4. The early years are important for development of '*basic skills*'. This is now an often-used expression that covers many things. Hence, it sounds good, but it is a very loose way of talking. However, it *does* mean that, as well as having lots to talk and to write about, the pupil will also have the skills associated with doing this. In other words, there will be an elementary grasp of number work, of sequence of numbers, of 'matching' one set with another, of adding and subtracting. And there will be an elementary grasp of such application of numbers to weight, to quantity, to time. This will be ele-

mentary, but a practical grasp of the concepts is important for subsequent development. Similarly, children will acquire a basic level of skill in numerous other domains: learning to construct a sentence, handle scissors and paintbrush, play with a ball in a game or sport, and sing the melody and words of a song.

5. There must be room for the directly *creative activities* reflected in its various artistic forms – drawing and painting, music making and playing, sculpting and modelling, dancing and miming. Not only do these activities give great pleasure in themselves – and not only do they require the acquisition and mastery of physical skills – they are important forms of 'making sense' of, and of communicating, the experience of the child. They meet very important, deep-down urges to create, which (unconsciously to the child) express, but make intelligible at the same time, the feelings that the child has.

The good infant classroom, therefore, will be a fairly lively room with many different activities going on, and with what can only be called a 'rich and stimulating environment'. There will be books. There will be a lot of talking. There will be objects to observe and to talk and write about. There will be artwork of the children on display. There will be a reading scheme, perhaps peculiar to the school. And what appears to be 'just play' will (under the good teachers) be purposeful play, requiring the acquisition of the basic skills of: reading and writing; talking and listening; discriminating texture, shape, and colour; sharing and co-operating.

### The junior stage

The arrangement of curriculum of the junior school is still usually class rather than subject based – one teacher will take the whole class for almost everything. That is not to say that there is no role for specialist teachers, but often these will have a leadership role within the school. The class teacher may not be an expert in music, but, guided by the music specialist, he or she can make a valuable contribution to the class's musical education. And sometimes one teacher may take other classes for physical education or for art. None the less, the junior school teacher is normally seen to be a 'generalist'.

Such a generalist approach to teaching does not entail that there should be no specialist rooms; but often primary schools are too small and too poorly provided for to allow for separate art, music, and environmental study spaces. They have to make do as best they can with non-specialist space for a growing specialisation in the approach to learning.

Think back to Chapter 1. Different government and HMI publications began to spell out (piecemeal, maybe, but a detailed account has emerged) broad principles upon which we should think about the curriculum. There should be balance and depth. There should be systematic planning over the years so that there might be continuity and progression. The curriculum in the early years must lay the foundations for the curriculum in later schooling. The secondary schools need to be able to assume certain skills, knowledge, attitudes and understandings.

The junior phase, therefore, sees the beginnings of these distinctive curriculum areas which are already there implicitly at the infant phase, and that will subsequently manifest themselves in a subject-based curriculum at the secondary stage. A parent should be able to go to a junior school and ask for the schemes of work in language development (and should be able to expect a detailed policy statement of how reading, writing and oral activities are seen to progress through the four or five years); in mathematical development; in the arts; in the humanities; in science.

One must be careful here. First, it is quite possible (indeed, many would say desirable) that there should be such policies without a curriculum fragmented into quite separate subjects. There should be a language policy *across* the curriculum (see page 16 where I refer to the Bullock Report); there should be the development of mathematical skills in the context of environmental studies or artwork. Secondly, for much of the time the pupils will be working co-operatively in teams on topics that are of interest to them, and that provide an integrating base for the learning within language, mathematics, science, humanities and the arts. Thirdly, there is always a danger, in pursuing too assiduously policy statements within specific areas, of forgetting those broader educational concerns of personal and social development so important to the infant teacher. Fourthly, there will be *progression* in this differentiation. The 7- and 8-year-olds will have a much more integrated timetable than the 10- or 11-year-olds (or the 12-year-olds in the middle school). Fifthly, much of the academic-sounding work (like science, say) will be performed in a very active way – in the context, possibly, of environmental studies in which general scientific principles will be demonstrated in a very concrete form.

In 'A View of the Curriculum', HMI shows the distinctive features of the junior stage with regard to the development of reading as follows:

By the age of 8 most children should be able to read, with confidence, simple sentences about familiar situations. More able 8 year olds should be expected to recall the theme of a short story they have read, as well as to comprehend books of information of the kind written for young children, while gifted children of this age should be able to use adult material, at least in part.

Once children have acquired the early reading skills, they should begin to learn to predict what may appear next in a piece of writing, to use various contextual clues, to develop and extend their reading vocabulary and to use dictionaries. They should also learn how to use the contents pages of a book and its index, and the ways in which books are arranged on library shelves. These skills need to be developed in a reading context that continually underlines the pleasure and advantage that can come from reading.

By the age of 11 many pupils should be aware of the more advanced skills of reading though these require continuing development during the secondary school years if the needs of more subject-based studies are to be met. Children need to learn to read books in a variety of ways, learning how to skim and sift material, to vary the pace of reading, to process information and to discriminate between the more and the less important features. Pupils need generally to increase their range and rate of comprehension which, in turn, requires an increasing commitment to sustained reading for which the school should make due provision.

With regard to mathematics, the continuity through the infant and junior stages is as follows:

Between the ages of 5 and 8 children should begin work in the following areas:

i.    the development of appropriate language; qualitative description, the recognition of objects from description; discriminating, classifying and sorting of objects; identifying objects and describing them unambiguously.

ii.    The recognition of common, simple mathematical relationships, both numerical and spatial; reasoning and logical deduction in connection with everyday things, geometrical shapes, number arrangements in order, etc.

iii.    The ability to describe quantitatively: the use of number in counting, describing, estimating and approximating.

iv.    The understanding of whole numbers and their relationships with one another.

v.    The appreciation of the measures in common use; sensible estimation using the appropriate units; the ability to measure length, weight, volume and capacity, area, time, angle and temperature to an everyday level of accuracy.

vi.    The understanding of money, contributing to a sense of the value of money, and the ability to carry out sensible purchases.

vii.    The ability to carry out practical activities involving the ideas of addition, subtraction, multiplication and division.

viii.    The ability to perform simple calculations involving the mathematical processes indicated by the signs $+$, $-$, $\times$, $\div$ with whole numbers (maintaining rapid recall of the sums, differences and products of pairs of numbers from 0 to 10).

ix.    The ability to check whether the result of a calculation is reasonable.

x.    The ability to use and interpret simple forms of diagrams, maps and tabulated information.

xi.    An appreciation of two- and three-dimensional shapes and their relationships with one another. The ability to recognise simple properties; to handle, create, discuss and describe them with confidence and appreciate spatial relationships, symmetry and similarity.

xii.  An ability to write clearly, to record mathematics in statements, neatly and systematically.

Before the age of 8 for some, but between the ages of 8 and 11 for most, children should continue to develop in these directions, and progress to:

i.  The appreciation of place value, the number system and number notation, including whole numbers, decimal fractions and vulgar fractions. The ability to recognise simple number patterns (odds and evens, multiples, divisors, squares, etc).

ii.  The ability to carry out with confidence and accuracy simple examples in the four operations of number, including two places of decimals as for pounds and pence and the measures as used.

iii.  The ability to approximate.

iv.  A sound understanding of place value applied to the decimal notation for numbers. The ability to carry out the addition and subtraction of numbers with up to two decimal places and the multiplication and division of such numbers by whole numbers up to and including 9.

v.  The multiplication and division of numbers with up to two decimal places by 10 and 100.

vi.  An appreciation of the connections between fractions, decimal fractions and the most common percentages.

vii.  The ability to use fractions in the sequence $\frac{1}{2}$, $\frac{1}{4}$, $\frac{1}{8}$, $\frac{1}{16}$, or $\frac{1}{3}$, $\frac{1}{6}$, $\frac{1}{12}$ or $\frac{1}{5}$, $\frac{1}{10}$, including the idea of equivalence in the discussion of everyday experiences.

viii.  An appreciation of the broader aspects of number, such as bases other than 10 and easy tests of divisibility.

ix.  An ability to read with understanding mathematics from books, and to use appropriate reference skills.

A number of children of this age will be capable of more advanced work, and they should be encouraged to undertake it.

Perhaps this developmental progress through infant to junior stages was most effectively described in a Schools Council project *Science 5 to 13*. This project attempted to match learning experience (and thereby teaching objectives) to the different stages of children's development. Of course, it had to start with justifying the point of teaching science, the distinctive nature of this part of the curriculum. (Yes, even at the infant stage, although science would not appear as a 'subject' within the infant programme.)

The project established a general aim of science education that would guide the establishment of objectives throughout the infant–junior stages. That was to 'develop an enquiring mind and a scientific approach to problems'. Such an aim could be broken down into eight general objectives (see Figure 2.2).

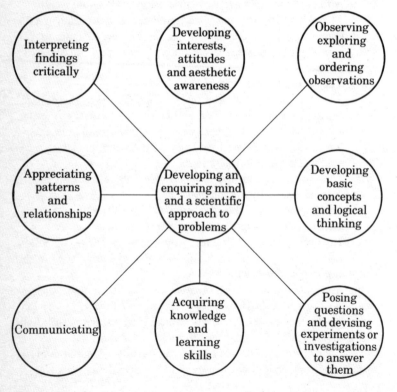

**Figure 2.2**

(Reprinted from Schools Council Science 5/13 Project, *Structures and Forces*, Macdonald Educational, 1972)

These general objectives are then spelt out in more specific ways in different topic areas. The following is an example within the important 'topic area' of 'structures'.

Quite early infants will have built with blocks or boxes and they will have sensed the effect of gravity and developed some idea about stability. Some will have tried to construct with other materials (paper and card, wood and fabrics particularly) and will have learnt by experience some of their limitations and possibilities. They will have looked at houses and cranes and trees, talked about them, made models and painted pictures.

So perhaps we could list some objectives attained as follows (even though these statements may appear rather coldly analytical for what goes on in infant schools).

Enjoyment in using all the senses for exploring and discrimination.
Willingness to collect material for observation and investigation.
Appreciation of the variety of living things and materials in the environment.
Awareness of the meaning of words which describe various types of quantity.
Ability to find answers to simple problems by investigation.
Ability to make comparisons in terms of one property or variable.
Ability to discriminate between different materials.

**Stage 1 objectives**
Generally speaking, the children concerned will be at the beginning of the junior school.

The Unit will take a closer look at the methods, materials, tools and machinery used in building. Why bricks are laid as they are, the value of the mortar, the form and strength of frameworks, arches, buttresses, cantilevers and suspension bridges could be some of the things leading to a knowledge of the directions in which forces act and the way they balance one another.

'The wind, blowing where it listeth, pushes on my chimney pots but the chimney pots, bless them, push back at the wind just as hard, and that is why they don't fall off.' J. E. Gordon, *The New Science of Strong Materials* (Pelican).

Looking at shapes will lead to experiments on strong and weak shapes, and the fact that strength depends on shape as well as on material.

41

Many variables are involved in bridge designing. For example, wind forces must be considered as well as the weight of the structure and the load of the traffic. There will be a great deal of model making, much for pleasure but some at least to answer questions (eg why don't the balconies fall off tall blocks of flats?), and some to experience qualities of materials or the way forces go (eg actually bridging a gap, or making a large structure from paper).

Measuring will become increasingly important in these problems. Arbitrary units of length, area, volume, weight and force will most likely be satisfactory for much of the work.

There will be a good deal of observation of structure pattern in living things and non-living things (eg birds' nests, spiders' webs, wire netting, etc).

So some objectives we could hope to achieve would be:

Interest in comparing and classifying living and non-living things.
Recognition of common shapes – square, circle and triangle.
Awareness of the structure and form of living things.
Recognition of the action of force.
Formation of the notions of horizontal and vertical.
Development of concepts of conservation of length and substance.
Awareness that more than one variable is involved in a particular change.
Knowledge of differences in properties between and within common groups of materials.
Skill in manipulating tools and materials.
Appreciation that properties of materials influence their use.

### Stage 2 objectives

The observations of structures will be more detailed (eg flying buttresses in churches, the design of motorway bridges, the balance of forces in a tower crane). The models will certainly continue. Measurement will become more accurate with the use of recognised units. The properties of materials considered will be more intangible than those which are appreciated readily by the senses (such as roughness, weight, bendability) and will involve experimental testing, for instance of the strengths of concrete or of wires.

There will be further observation on structure and form in living things, now more related to function and including structure visible with a good hand-lens.

The effect of structures, such as cities, or dams, on the natural balance of life ought to be dealt with.

Some objectives at this stage would be:

Preference for putting ideas to the test before accepting or rejecting them.

Awareness of internal structure in living and non-living things.

Recognition of similar and congruent shapes.

Awareness of symmetry in shapes and structures.

Ability to classify living things and non-living things in different ways.

Ability to visualise objects from different angles and the shape of cross-sections.

Development of concepts of conservation of weight, area and volume.

Ability to use representational models for investigating problems or relationships.

Familiarity with a wide range of forces and ways in which they can be changed.

Ability to measure properties of materials.

Ability to construct models as a means of recording observations.

Awareness of the impact of man's activities on other living things.

Appreciation of how the form and structure of materials relate to their function and properties.

I have, therefore, illustrated briefly from English, mathematics and science how one might begin to think and to plan developmentally from 5 to 11 or 12 – and how already there are several interesting examples of this. Once we move into the secondary stage, however, there often seems a major break with what has gone on before.

### Secondary stage

When children progress to a secondary school, usually at the age of 11, the change seems immense. From a school where they are looked after for most of the time by one teacher who will know them very well indeed, they move to another school where they will, in the course of the week, meet many teachers who are the subject specialists. Sometimes they will move around from one part of the school to another – from geography room to science laboratories – as the curriculum is seen as an aggregate of specialist areas of study. And this can seem bewildering to the 11-year-old – as well as posing problems for looking after personal possessions and equipment.

This is not always the case. Some schools feel they want to extend the best of primary-school practice into the secondary school, at least for the first year, so that there is a class teacher for several subjects and so that there is the minimum of movement about the school. None the less, this does remain an important curriculum issue: the extent to which the secondary-school timetable should be split up into quite separate subjects of the kind many grammar-schooled parents would recognise from their own youth or, alternatively, based in part around activities or themes or integrated areas.

Furthermore, there is usually a major break in the progressive development of the secondary curriculum. The final two years are seen as the preparation for the examinations at 16+. It has, therefore, been a time when students need to be separated into different examination groups – the more able pursuing courses for GCE O level, the less able being put into CSE or other examination classes. To some extent, this is no longer necessary because of the new GCSE examination. But 'differentiation' is required in some subjects.

One way in which this differentiation takes place is through an options system, although this is normally justified in terms of the value of giving choice to pupils. In Years 4 and 5 there will be a common core of studies (usually English, mathematics, physical education, religious education) plus a range of option lists which will be so organised as to ensure a balanced curriculum.

Therefore, a typical secondary school curriculum may look something like this.

### Years 1 to 3

There is, of course, immense variety among the many secondary schools, but beneath this is a certain general framework that most of them seem to share. HMI carries out regular visits on schools and publishes reports. From a random selection of these reports, it would seem that, for the first three years, most secondary schools would have a timetable that looked very like Table 2.1:

**Table 2.1**

| Year 1 | Year 2 | Year 3 |
|---|---|---|
| Tutorial & PSE* | Tutorial & PSE* | Tutorial & PSE* |
| English | English | English |
| Humanities [History, geography, social studies] | | |
| RE | RE | RE |
| Modern languages | Modern languages | Modern languages |
| Maths | Maths | Maths |
| Science [Physics, chemistry, biology] | | |
| CDT [Woodwork, metalwork, design, technology, home economics, needlework] | | |
| Creative arts [Art, music, drama, dance] | | |
| PE | PE | PE |

* Personal and social education

There are several features of Table 2.1 that need to be drawn to the reader's attention.

1. Students are normally put into form-groups in which they are registered for morning and afternoon classes, records about them are maintained, and general 'pastoral care' and discipline are dealt with. The form tutor, therefore, is a key person in the general guidance and help that need to be given to students. Very often in the past, these form meetings have been merely a way of getting through the necessary bureaucratic business, such as registration. But, in the past few years, they have often assumed a much greater educational significance. They have, in other words, become part of the curricu-

lum, with planned activities aimed at helping the students work in groups, develop personal and social skills, explore matters of personal concern, and seek guidance and counselling. Personal and social education (PSE) now has a place on the secondary-school curriculum either through these tutorial periods or through a subject called Personal and Social Education.

The following is a way in which such a 'subject', or programme of personal and social education, might develop through the school (see L. Button, *Developing Group Work*, Hodder & Stoughton, 1981, p. 3).

## Main Themes

There are a number of main themes running through the programmes for the five years. The themes are picked up with differing intensity as the programme proceeds, according to the age and development of the young people. The effort to be devoted to the themes can be seen from the schedules which precede the programmes for each half term. The main themes are as follows.

*The Pupil's Place in the School.* There is an emphasis on a responsible contribution to and an active participation in the affairs of the school. It is important that pupils of all ages should feel involved, but the way in which this involvement is expressed needs to correspond to the age of the young people.

*The Pastoral Group as a Small Caring Community.* This is the basis upon which everything else is built. Support also involves challenges: support must not be confused with cosiness. The group needs to work out its own caring programme, and the tutor will need to help the young people to establish the style in which this is approached.

*Relationships, the Self and Social Skills.* Although this heading covers a very large area of concern, these elements are put together since they are so interdependent. The term 'relationships' is wide-ranging, including friendship, other peers, family, other adults and people in authority. The development of social skills and self-knowledge is approached with increasing sophistication as the experience of the young people grows.

*Communication Skills.* Very rapid progress can be made here. Being articulate includes being able to identify the internal concerns and issues that are waiting to be expressed. The skill of active listening and an interest in the other person underlies so much in life.

*School Work and Study Skills*. Which are the areas of skill and concern that are common to all school work, and can reasonably be dealt with within the pastoral programme? This section is especially concerned with attitudes, anxieties and objectives, and with group support in moving towards those objectives.

*Academic Guidance and Careers Education*. This is an attempt to help young people to know themselves and to move towards wise decisions. It is not about ready-made advice: the initiative should be in the hands of the young people. The discussion of careers should be very much an educational programme about the world of work and other people's lives, and not narrowly about the job that young people may take up.

*Health and Hygiene*. Much of the total programme can be regarded as 'Health Education'; this section is more especially about health and hygiene. In most secondary schools some of the information included in subject areas contributes to health education, and it is important that there should be some co-ordination of effort in this respect.

*Personal Interests*. This is about pursuits and leisure interests that young people can follow outside school, especially those that can be continued after leaving school. Here also there will be a need for liaison with other departments in the school.

2. The 'subjects' have been listed in a particular order so that the reader might understand different ways in which schools could regroup them. For example, English or a modern language or RE is sometimes seen to be part of a humanities faculty; maths, science, and craft, design and technology (CDT) of the science faculty; alternatively, CDT and creative arts part of the creative arts faculty.

3. Within the broad categories, different subject divisions or integrations might be found. Thus, for example, within the humanities there might be an integrated, topic-based course, with only a gradual differentiation (if at all) into the component subjects of history, geography and social studies. Or, within the sciences, there is increasingly an integrated-science

course, only rarely differentiated into separate subjects of physics, chemistry and biology. (This is partly due to the lack of qualified physicists and chemists.) Or, again, within the creative arts, there may be an integrated course. But much more likely is a 'taster' course at first in each of the main arts areas, followed by selection of one or two of them. In art, for example, children might spend a few weeks doing painting, then try their hand at sculpture, next at ceramics, later at graphic design, to gain some experience of different ways of expressing and developing their artistic talent.

4. Design and technology is an increasingly important subject, but it might be integrated with science or it might transform the old skills-based approach in the crafts of woodwork and metalwork.

5. And where is information technology (IT) in all this? The use of microcomputers, word processors and the like has become an important part of adult life. There are various options. One is to teach it as a subject – added on to all the rest in a crowded timetable. Another is to 'integrate' it with each subject, seeing IT as a learning tool (just as reading or writing is) that is employed across the curriculum.

6. The degree of differentiation or integration, and the exact quantity of time given to the different subjects, are partly dependent on the following organisational factors. Some schools stream pupils from the very beginning – that is, they put the pupils in groups according to general ability. Others believe in mixed-ability groups. And there is a wide range of possibilities in between: banding (or putting pupils into two or three broad bands of ability); setting (or putting pupils into ability groups for particular subjects – often mathematics and foreign languages); or doing any one of these only in certain years. In making distinctions between types of pupil, the school sometimes feels able to allow some to take a second foreign language, or to insist that some (but not all) follow an integrated-science course.

*Years 4 and 5*

Many secondary schools choose to adopt a core-plus-options system. Often it was justified on the basis of the need to give students a much greater choice, which would enable them to find what they were interested in. It would enable them also to alter the balance of the curriculum somewhat, without it being altogether unbalanced. Thus, a budding scientist (see the highly simplified Table 2.2) would be able to take three separate sciences, and yet maintain breadth within the other areas of experience. On the other hand, a less able scientist might choose just one science or integrated science, while studying a second foreign language. Such a system also enabled the less academically able young person to take up more practical and vocationally oriented subjects – leading possibly to quite different qualifications.

**Table 2.2**

| | | | |
|---|---|---|---|
| C | PSE + Tutorial + RE | | |
| O | English | | |
| R | Mathematics | | |
| E | PE | | |
| | One subject from each of the six lists of options | | |
| O | 1. Physics | Integrated science | Music |
| P | 2. Chemistry | Music | Vocational preparation |
| T | 3. Biology | Modern languages | Typing |
| I | 4. Modern languages | Geography | Social studies |
| O | 5. Art | Music | Drama |
| N | 6. History | CDT | Computer studies |

The options system, however, was also a convenient way of streaming pupils without that word being used. Thus the less academically able would be advised into a particular package of options.

An option system can be very complicated and hard for the parent to understand. In some cases, such a system might contain as many as 30 or more subjects. The larger the school, then the greater the variety that might be offered. But a small school has to reduce the options and expand the core. Indeed, there are schools which now offer no option system at all.

New demands are now made upon the school, and these have become known as cross-curriculum themes or activities – information technology, health education (including, very often, sex education), economic awareness, careers guidance. There are various strategies for including these. They may be added to the core subjects, in particular to the PSE slot, or some might be integrated into the way learning is engaged in across the curriculum.

## Pre-vocational education

The traditional shape and content of the curriculum in secondary schools received a serious challenge from a quite unexpected quarter in 1982. One major criticism of schools was that they were not preparing students well enough for the future, particularly for the world of work. The Department of Employment, therefore, through the agency of the Manpower Services Commission (MSC), launched the Technical and Vocational Education Initiative (TVEI) in schools, for pupils aged from 14 to 18.

TVEI, in effect, was a large sum of money given to pilot schools, eventually in nearly every LEA, to establish a curriculum that could meet the following criteria:

- promote equal opportunities;
- provide a four-year curriculum designed as a preparation for adult life in a society liable to rapid change;
- encourage initiative, problem-solving and other aspects of personal development;
- contain a vocational element throughout;
- relate technical and vocational elements to potential employment opportunities;

- plan work experience within the programme;
- establish links with subsequent training and educational opportunities;
- include regular careers and educational assessment;
- prepare students for one or more nationally recognised qualifications;
- design courses so that they might be usefully replicated.

There were many different schemes from which many lessons can be learnt. But what they had in common were:

- a change in styles of teaching and learning (much more practical and experiential with an emphasis on team-work);
- a change in ways in which we assess young people and record their achievement;
- closer links with the community, especially with employers through work experience and mini-enterprise schemes;
- increased use of technology, especially information technology, as an aid to learning;
- a stress upon guidance and counselling as an essential link between school and subsequent training and employment.

This initiative is now being extended to all schools, although on a much smaller budget. This quite radical change in secondary education reflects different influences and pressures – from government, from teachers, from employers, from parents and from the students themselves. And it reflects, too, a different response to the context in which education and training are taking place. What is emerging is a reappraisal of the purposes that education should serve and of the values that it should embody.

Of course, this reappraisal could take different directions, since there is a political context to education. But the more generous view of educational change that pre-vocational education represents could be described as one that:

- encourages a *shift of responsibility for learning* from teacher to student (thereby challenging traditional teaching styles

51

and requiring the learner to develop skills of independent enquiry);

- makes learning more *project and activity based*;
- relates what is learnt to *future needs* of the students and of society (whether or not these are employment needs);
- links educational programmes more closely to *community resources* (including employers, parents and other institutions of learning);
- focuses upon *personal development and effectiveness* (thus stressing the importance of guidance and counselling);
- sees the central value of the *creative arts and humanities* in meeting those personal needs;
- introduces the student to the *principles and practices of technology*;
- develops *social, economic, and political awareness*;
- recognises the overriding importance of *communication skills*;
- promotes *equal opportunities* for people of different race, sex and class.

Education is thus becoming much more concerned with the process of learning than with covering a syllabus; more concerned with individual needs than with homogeneous groups; and yet (paradoxically enough) more concerned with the economic and social needs of society than simply with the progression of individuals.

### 'The Curriculum 5 to 16'

The HMI booklet 'The Curriculum 5 to 16' (number 2 in its Curriculum Matters series) attempts an overview of the infant, junior and secondary stages.

*Aims:*

1. the development of lively minds;
2. the acquisition of knowledge and skills relevant to the future;

3. the development of literacy and numeracy;
4. the 'instilling' of moral values;
5. the development of social and scientific awareness;
6. the appreciation of human achievements and aspirations.

*The curriculum:*

All those activities designed to achieve those aims – including, therefore the 'extra curriculum' activities, such as residential visits, or the ways in which teachers relate to pupils (the ethos of the school).

*Framework:*

1. Areas of learning and experience:
   - aesthetic and creative: 'the capacity to respond emotionally and intellectually to sensory experience; the awareness of degrees of quality; and the appreciation of beauty and fitness for purpose'.
   - human and social: understanding of how people live, of their relationships with each other and with their environment, and with how human action has influenced events and conditions.
   - linguistic and literacy: 'increasing pupils' command of language in listening, speaking, reading and writing' – partly to be achieved through various uses of language, partly through the specific study of language and literature.
   - mathematical: learning 'a variety of mathematical concepts and processes "necessary" to understand and appreciate relationships and pattern in both numbers and space in their everyday lives . . .'.
   - moral: the understanding of concepts such as fairness and justice, and the formation and testing of moral convictions.
   - physical: the development of control, co-ordination and mobility and of manipulative and motor skills, plus knowledge about the human body.

- scientific: knowledge and understanding of the natural world and the capacity to engage in systematic enquiry (observing, selecting from observations, framing hypotheses, devising and conducting experiments).
- spiritual: developing 'feelings and convictions about the significance of human life and the world as a whole which pupils may experience within themselves and meet at secondhand in their study of the world and the way of life of other people'.
- technological: the knowledge and abilities connected with controlling events and ordering our environment.

2. Elements of learning:
- knowledge: content to be learnt;
- concepts: generalisations and principles that organise knowledge;
- skills: the capacity and competence to perform a task (in communication, observation, study, problem-solving, practical movement, creativity, number, and personal and social relationships);
- attitudes: the overt expression of values and personal qualities.

*Principles for shaping the curriculum as a whole:*

1. Breadth: contact with the nine areas of learning defined above.
2. Balance: appropriate attention given over a period of time to each area of learning and to each element of learning.
3. Relevance: seen by the pupils to meet present and prospective needs (which will include, for the secondary ones, the relationship to employment).
4. Differentiation: relating approximately to the different ability and motivational needs of the range of students.
5. Progression and continuity: coherence from stage to stage in planning and experience from 5 to 16.

*Assessment:*

There should be, in tandem with curriculum design, a system of assessment that enables a record of progress to be maintained and learning difficulties to be recognised and diagnosed.

In other books within the series, HMI spelt out what the application of this model would look like subject by subject. These, listed in the appendix, pages 112–3, should be read by parent, governor, or general reader who is interested in any specific subject.

## General principles and conclusion

The curriculum is made up of the arrangements made by a school so that the children learn. Often its parents and governors will see it as a timetable full of subject headings. But, of course, it is much more than that.

A properly conceived curriculum has some vision, some aims that explain the kind of learning that the school wants to take place. A school should have aims that have been thought through and reflected upon and that show the philosophy and the values of the school.

More than that, however; the school should be able to show how those aims are translated into practice – into year-by-year and week-by-week organisation. The curriculum should not be too detailed; that would detract from the flexibility and from the responsiveness to individual need that education requires. But, on the other hand, it should be possible to see programmes of work which reflect the gradual, bit by bit, attainment of knowledge, understanding, skills and attitudes necessary to fulfil the aims. Only in that way can there be assurance of progression and continuity.

The place of 'subjects' is important in the development of these programmes of work. After all, subjects are ways in which we have come to organise knowledge, skills and understanding. To be a scientist, you have to think and to address problems in a certain way – formulating a hypothesis, testing it out, looking for alternative explanations. But you also need eventually to acquire certain ideas or concepts that enable you to get beneath surface appearances and to explain things more systematically – concepts like 'force', 'energy', 'inertia', for instance. A programme of study should show how, gradually, these ways of enquiring and these concepts enter into the curriculum design. It will show the topics and projects through which they arise. It will show, desirably, how the pupils will be assessed – but with a view to finding out whether teaching has been successful, and, if not, what went wrong (what learning difficulties the child has).

Therefore, a parent or governor or LEA adviser or a visiting HMI ought, in getting to grips with the curriculum of a school, be able to ask for the various programmes that demonstrate continuity and progression in the acquisition of concepts, knowledge and skills in different areas. These areas have been suggested by HMI. You may object in detail, but in general there is little challenge to this way of ensuring breadth and balance.

Such programmes need to provide key concepts and major stages in that progression – not lots of detail, for there needs to be room for treating differently children with different abilities and motivations. Children can grasp a concept – let us say, that of 'reproduction' or that of 'social interdependence' – at different levels of complexity. You do not expect an 8-year-old to have the same understanding of the laws of gravity as a bright 16-year-old.

One can see, therefore, the temptation 'to go national' on such programmes of work. First, as children move from school to school it would be useful if some uniformity in learning targets could be assured. Secondly, if a programme is (in such general terms) right for one group of children, then surely it would seem right for another group. Thirdly, it would help parents and governors to know what is happening, and to be able to raise sensible questions to teachers. Fourthly, it would ensure that the best that is thought and said (in, say, government reports such as the Bullock, Cockcroft, Warnock,

Kingman or Swann – see pages 16–21) can be more easily transferred to the curriculum of all our children.

There are, however, very real reasons for anxiety. First, the shape and content of the curriculum are ultimately determined by the values or aims that direct our efforts. And it is clear from what has been said that there is no consensus on what those are. Is everyone convinced that we should be promoting lively and enquiring minds – even if such minds come up with beliefs and values that we do not like? And is there agreement that education before the age of 16 should have a vocational, work-related orientation? If so, how much of this should there be?

Secondly, the role of subjects remains controversial. We can see from the papers 'The School Curriculum' and 'A Framework for the Curriculum' (see pages 22–3) that the DES tends to see the organisation of the curriculum as, in essence, an aggregate of subjects. But HMI tend to talk about 'areas of experience' to which subjects make a contribution. And the 'pre-vocational movement' (see page 50) starts from a very different angle, namely, the personal needs of young people as they prepare psychologically as well as economically for a difficult future. In addition, there remain demands from the vocational pressure group for more specific, work-related objectives, arising from an analysis of what industry and commerce need.

Thirdly, a National Curriculum, albeit attractive on the surface and already operating in many other countries, might not be as responsive to individual needs. There is a very strong curriculum tradition (which is alive and well in many primary schools) that learning arises best from the concerns and interests of the learner. The good teacher is highly creative and imaginative in building on the experience that the child brings into school. Such experience and interests will be different from locality to locality, from family to family and from child to child. Of course, an eye has to be kept on broader educational goals; a bridge has to be established between personal needs and the cultural resources that the school puts at the disposal of the child. None the less, such a teacher would not want to be too constrained by a programme imposed from outside.

The way ahead therefore is not easy. In the next two chapters we shall see how the government has tackled the problem.

# Part Two
# AFTER THE ACT

# Chapter 3

# CHANGING CONTROL OF EDUCATION AND THE CURRICULUM

The Education Reform Act became law on 29 July 1988. It is the most important piece of educational legislation since the 1944 Education Act. It aims to meet the criticisms of the educational system, particularly of the schools, that were referred to in Part One of this book.

The best-known aspect of the Act concerns the National Curriculum, which is the main focus of this book and which I will explain in the next chapter. But, as I showed in Part One, you cannot divorce questions about curriculum from those about management of, and responsibility for, schools and what they do. And the Act has had a great deal to say about that.

## The major proposals of the Act

### 'Open admissions' (Part I, Chapter 2)

This part of the Act gives parents the right to choose the school their children should go to – up to the physical capacity of the school to take the children (its capacity, generally speaking, in 1978–79 before the declining school population affected the numbers of children that had to be provided for).

The importance of this part of the Act is that LEAs no longer have the powers to plan the provision of education across the system, protecting the unpopular school against the steady erosion of numbers which will eventually affect the capacity of the school to provide a balanced, broad, relevant and differentiated curriculum – meeting the needs of all children 'according to age, ability, and aptitude' (see page 9). The government's justification for these clauses is that extending parental choice will make schools more responsive to consumer demand and more concerned to improve curriculum standards.

### 'Local financial management' (LFM) or Local management of schools (LMS) (Part I, Chapter 3)

This section provides for the school budgets to be devolved to the governors of schools with over 200 pupils. The budget will include the salaries of staff, the costs of maintaining the school on a daily basis (postage, telephones, heating, etc.) and the costs of resources needed for the curriculum (books, equipment, field-trips, etc.). The LEA retains certain areas of expenditure, such as the advisory and psychological service and the maintenance of the fabric of the school. The exact amount of the total cost devolved to the school will vary over the coming years, but will be around three-quarters of its total cost.

The implications for the management of the curriculum are immense. Schools must show their values and priorities in a way that was not previously possible – namely, in where they put their money. Should one replace a teacher with several computers? Should one pay extra to certain teachers because of their subject expertise, at the cost of much cheaper teaching elsewhere? And how much money should be spent on practical work (such as work-experience) rather than upon the more traditional school activities?

### Charges for school activities (Part I, Chapter 5)

The Act permits LEAs to charge for activities outside school hours – unless they are necessary for examination purposes. But charges are not permitted for activities within school hours, except in the cases of individual music tuition and board and lodging on educational field-trips.

There has been a lot of confusion caused by this section of the Act. Many schools enrich the curriculum with visits to museums, to art galleries, to the zoo, to the moors, or to the sea. These trips are possible only if the costs are paid by parents, although usually there is a way of assisting children of parents who cannot afford to pay. Indeed, the expansion of work-experience as an essential part of the curriculum for 15- or 16-year-olds depends upon parents in most cases paying the bus fares to and from the work-place. All such charges are now forbidden, and many schools must drop such valuable and enriching activities from the curriculum.

### Grant-maintained status or 'Opting out' (Part I, Chapter 4)

The Act provides for the governors of schools of more than 300 pupils to apply for 'grant-maintained status' (i.e. to opt out of the LEA system and to receive direct funding from the DES to the amount that they would have received had they remained within the LEA). The application must be approved by a majority of parents after a secret ballot.

The first governing bodies who made an application were mostly in schools which were under the threat of closure within the LEA's reorganisation plans. The success of the application depends upon agreement of the Secretary of State – it is by no means automatic, and it does change dramatically the control and the responsibility for the curriculum as described in Chapter 1.

### City technology colleges (CTC)

City technology colleges (CTC) were designed to be sponsored by industry. They are referred to as 'independent schools' in the Act, but in fact as much as 80 per cent of their capital and running costs will come from central government. They will be required to have a 'broad curriculum with an emphasis on science and technology' and will have to keep to 'the substance of the National Curriculum'. The first CTC opened in September 1988, in Solihull, and initially twenty were planned.

The significance of CTCs lies not so much in the curriculum stress upon science and technology (that has been the case in an increasing number of schools, especially as a result of TVEI, see page 50). Rather does it lie in the changing control of and responsibility for the curriculum. In this case it is being taken once again out of the hands of LEAs. Moreover, the lavishly resourced CTCs, with admissions of up to 1,000 students, must affect the resourcing of, the staffing of, and the admissions to neighbouring schools. The reason for establishing CTCs was said, by the government, to be the extension of parental choice, but the curriculum provision for all must be affected. In the early stages of negotiation, it became clear that many large firms were not willing to support a CTC, preferring to work with existing schools. Concern was also expressed when over three-quarters of the capital costs of building the Nottingham CTC was provided by the government instead of by industry.

### Inner London Education Authority (ILEA) (Part II)

The Act abolishes the ILEA from 1 April 1990, and the thirteen London boroughs assume responsibility for running their own education services. The Secretary of State will have the power to veto the appointment to a senior post of anyone he or she considers to be unsuitable.

This part of the Act is not of general concern. Nor is it immediately relevant to curriculum matters. But it does illustrate the changing control of education and the diminishing role of LEAs as they are asked to conform to central directives. The ILEA had been one of the most innovative authorities in developing the school curriculum.

### Further and higher education (Part II, Chapter 1, and Part IV)

The Act has several clauses affecting further and higher education that are very important in themselves, although only marginally relevant to the purposes of this book. The main proposals are: polytechnics to become semi-independent corporations, free from the control of LEAs; a University Funding Council to replace the University Grants Committee, with important powers to determine the conditions under which universities will receive funding – opening up the possibility of 'contract funding'; and an increase in the number of representatives from industry on the councils and governing bodies of universities, polytechnics and colleges of further education.

## Implications of these changes

To see all these changes separately would be to miss the point, for they add up to a consistent political initiative to alter how the curriculum should be organised, controlled and linked with the community.

First, the role of LEAs *is* diminished. They no longer have powers to maintain and develop *a system* of education to the same degree as previously. 'Open admission' removes the right from LEAs to ensure that schools remain viable educational entities, because the popularity of one school simply attracts a greater proportion of a diminishing school-age population, thus rendering the less popular schools incapable of providing the balanced curriculum that is desirable. 'Opting out' and the establishment of CTCs similarly have the effect of undermining systematic planning and of removing services from the LEA, for the smaller the number of schools under its control the smaller the resources (advisory, psychological, careers, etc.) that the LEA can have at its disposal. And LMS ensures the devolution of responsibility for running the educational service from the LEA to the governing bodies of schools. Moreover, as money becomes increasingly conditional upon meeting the requirements laid down by central government, there is less local control of the curriculum.

Secondly, responsibility has been shifted 'downwards' to reconstituted governing bodies that have a relatively large representation of parents and of the community who can promote the school, respond to local concerns, and make significant financial and management decisions that can affect the 'delivery' of the curriculum.

Thirdly, however, the vacuum created by the reduction of LEA power and responsibility has been filled substantially by central government, which is setting the detailed framework within which the governing bodies of schools have to operate. These, thus, are freed of LEA control, only to be constrained by central government.

Thus, there is now a strong centrally devised framework which regulates an otherwise open market within which there can be freedom of choice. In this way, it is thought, the problem of standards can be addressed. These are defined centrally, but monitored locally. And the spur to schools to match these standards with improved performance lies in the power of members of the local community to exercise their choice in a free market. A clear definition of standards and a proper labelling of the product is essential, so that the clients or consumers can be properly informed in exercising their choice. After all, the standard of tinned beans can be improved through consumer choice only if the potential purchaser has full knowledge of the ingredients.

There are inevitably misgivings that many people have over this changing control of the curriculum.

First, the quality of the curriculum does depend to some extent on the assurance of long-term funding for a school. The market context, in which the income of a school (and thus the curriculum that can be successfully followed) is subject to the short-term impact of fashion and consumer choice, seems inappropriate to the successful provision of education for all.

Secondly, in order to be popular, a school may find it inconvenient to have its fair share of children with special needs. After all, such children are more demanding of time and resources. They can deflate the figures of successful performance in public examination – the main measure whereby the consumers are going to evaluate the potential choices in the educational market.

Thirdly, we are swiftly moving towards a hierarchy of schools that might easily lead to a curriculum experience differentiated according to type of school rather than curriculum needs. Thus we have:

- totally independent schools;
- partly independent schools (i.e. those that receive government funding through the Assisted Places Scheme);
- city technology colleges (funded partly from industry, partly from the government);
- grant-maintained schools, in direct receipt of government

money, independent of LEAs, in control of own staffing, buildings, curriculum, maintenance, etc.;

- popular LEA-maintained schools – successful under the Open Admission system;
- unpopular LEA-maintained schools – often with a disproportionate number of young people with special needs that, under the laws of competition, have been excluded from the other schools.

Many people believe that this is not the best way to ensure an education for all according to age, ability and aptitude – or to maintain standards all round, or to ensure that the educational system meets the needs of the economy.

### Government powers

In the next chapter I shall describe the curriculum that the government has legislated in order to meet the criticisms and anxieties described earlier in the book. Such a curriculum is the outcome, as we have seen, of ten years of deliberation and slow development of a curriculum framework. The government felt confident, therefore, in ensuring that such a framework could be introduced forthwith. To do this, the Education Act provided for the following:

1. A National Curriculum Council (NCC) and the Curriculum Council for Wales (CCW) whose members will be appointed by the Secretary of State, which would oversee the implementation of the National Curriculum.

2. A Schools Examination and Assessment Council (SEAC), again whose members will be appointed by the Secretary of State, which would arrange for, and oversee, the testing of children at 7, 11, 14 and 16 in different Core and Foundation Subjects (see page 70).

3. The powers for the Secretary of State 'to make orders', following advice from the NCC, concerning:

- the definition of attainment targets;
- the programmes of study relating to these targets;

- the assessment arrangements for each of these attainment targets.

The practical implications of the 'powers to give orders' might be illustrated as follows. The Science Working Group initially produced an interim report on attainment targets, programmes of study and assessment arrangements. The proposals presupposed approximately 20 per cent of time being spent on science. The Secretary of State disagreed with this, and other conclusions of the report. He argued, for instance, for something nearer 12 per cent of the total time. The Secretary of State is entitled to reject the recommendations of working parties or of the National Curriculum Council. He is obliged to make public his reasons why, but is in no way subject to any obligation to accept the advice given. 'The Secretary of State may make the Order, with or without modifications' (Section 11). Therefore the Secretary would seem to have total power, though after consultation which may or may not be heeded.

4. The powers for the Secretary of State to issue regulations saying what kind of information is to be made available about schools, the curriculum, assessment arrangements, and the result of assessment.

The Secretary of State thus has greater powers under the 1988 Act for determining the general shape, the specific objectives and the programmes of study of the curriculum than any other previous Secretary or Minister of Education. Indeed, should a school wish to modify the programme of study – to try out a major innovation, say – special application will have to be made to the Secretary of State. Britain has long been noted, by contrast with its European partners, for a decentralised curriculum with responsibility firmly in the hands of the professionals. Clause 9 of the 1988 Act reversed that.

This, of course, complements a process that was begun with the reform of the 16+ examinations. Under the GCSE arrangements, the subject-specific criteria for all subjects have to be agreed by the Secretary of State. Under this Act, no external qualifications (for example, those by the RSA, by CGLI, or by BTEC) may be offered in maintained schools to pupils of compulsory school age unless approved by the Secretary of State. (Similar *reserve* powers are provided in the Act for qualifications offered to all up to the age of 19 on full-time education.)

These then are the *organisational* arrangements and the context for the introduction of the *National Curriculum*. If parents happen not to like them, or that which is being 'ordered', then of course they can show their disapproval by 'opting out' or choosing the independent sector, whether or not subsidised by the Assisted Places Scheme.

## Chapter 4

# THE NATIONAL CURRICULUM 5 TO 16

The most important piece of the 1988 legislation, as far as many people are concerned, was the National Curriculum. The possibility of a *national* curriculum was hardly dreamed of only a few years ago. But it should have been clear from the documents referred to in Chapter 1 that the government intended to direct, much more than it had done previously, what should be taught in schools. Not only was it laying down general principles (breadth, balance, relevance, progression and differentiation); not only was it keeping LEAs on their toes by asking for detailed accounts of curriculum policies; not only was it initiating a range of curriculum innovations, such as TVEI: it was also prescribing the aims of the curriculum, the framework within which these aims were to be pursued, and the subjects (including the amount of time to be devoted to them) which should fill up that framework. None the less, it came as a surprise when the government finally published its Consultation Paper – the Red Book – in July 1987, setting out what it thought the National Curriculum should contain.

The consultation period was brief – August and September 1987. Nevertheless, 15,000 responses were elicited. Be that as it may, the final Act differed only in minor details from the proposals in the Consultation Paper. I shall, therefore, confine my account to what finally passed into legislation, which will be purely descriptive. More critical issues will be raised later.

### Foundation Subjects (Part I, Chapter 1)

There are four critical and interrelated aspects of these curriculum proposals.

1. There is a list of *Core and Foundation Subjects*, although it is not entirely clear what is the significance of the distinction between Core and Foundation. All are prescribed:

*Core*:
- English
- Mathematics
- Science
- Welsh (at Welsh-speaking schools)

*Foundation*:
- History
- Geography
- Art
- Music
- Technology
- Physical education
- Modern foreign language
- Welsh (at non-Welsh-speaking Welsh schools)

Religious education was omitted from the Consultation Paper. It has now become part of the 'basic curriculum', but not a Foundation Subject. The reason for this is that, although it remains, under the 1944 Education Act which has not been repealed, a subject required to be taught by law, its interpretation (or what will go on under that title) will be determined by local agreements, not by central direction.

The first thing to note about the National Curriculum is that it is essentially an aggregate of quite separate subjects and that these subjects provide no surprises. Indeed, the list is not dissimilar from that of the 1904 Regulations for secondary schools. The government's perception of the curriculum has not changed in a significant way in over 80 years, despite the many exciting developments that have taken place both within and outside school. The main exception to this is 'technology', although music, too, has been added to art ('drawing' in 1904) and reference to gender differences has been dropped (housewifery for girls and manual work for boys in 1904).

It is possible for individual schools to apply for exemption from the National Curriculum to enable them to engage in innovative work that is of general interest, but (as explained in the last chapter) only if permission of the Secretary of State is given.

Secondly, a National Curriculum Council (NCC) for England and a Curriculum Council for Wales (CCW) were established to keep the curriculum under review, to advise the Secretary of State on research and development, and to publish information. The National Curriculum Council is in York. It has a key role in agreeing the details of the National Curriculum.

Thirdly, the National Curriculum should take up about 70 to 80 per cent of the timetable – there will remain a fair amount of time for additional or expanded activities or subjects.

2. Within each Foundation Subject, *attainment targets* will be set at ages 7, 11, 14 and 16. In other words, the government will say what children ought to be able to do and to think at these different ages. Working parties have been established to decide what these targets should be in English, maths, science and technology and they have published their first reports. The idea is that there should be specified in these (and eventually in the other) Core and Foundation Subjects desirable achievements from Level 1 to Level 10, each level saying what children should be able to do. They are, therefore, 'criterion-referenced'. Needless to say, many teachers do not like this – it seems a slight on their competence. But others (and parents) may prefer the clearer targets – the goals to which one might work in a developmental sequence. Thus by 7, children will normally be expected to have reached Level 1, 2 or 3, by 11 Level 3, 4, 5 or 6, by 14 Level 4, 5, 6, 7 or 8, and by 16 Level 5, 6, 7, 8, 9 and 10. Higher levels will thus incorporate lower levels in a developmental sequence.

3. In association with these attainment targets, there will be prescribed *programmes of study*. These will be introduced subject by subject over a period of years. Before they are prescribed 'by order of Parliament', there will be consultation periods to permit wider consideration by subject associations,

and others, of the proposals. But the Secretary of State reserves the right to ignore the advice given.

4. Pupils will be *assessed* in each subject towards the end of the school year in which most children in the class reach 7, 11, 14 and 16 – although it may be the case that exceptions will be made of certain subjects at the age of 7. The results of the assessments of *individual* pupils will be made available only to the pupils' parents, to the governors or to the LEA. On the other hand, the general performance of the schools in terms of pupils' performance will be made generally available, thus enabling comparisons to be made between schools. There is a new School Examinations and Assessment Council (SEAC) to review assessment and examinations, and to arrange for moderation of assessment.

Although several years are needed to reach agreement on attainment targets and programmes of study, all schools were expected to teach all Core and Foundation Subjects and RE from autumn 1989. It was a very rapid introduction compared with the longer time-scale of many other countries, because just thirteen months elapsed between the 1988 Act becoming law and schools being required to teach the National Curriculum.

## Timetable for implementing the National Curriculum

The government moved very quickly in the implementation of the National Curriculum. Interim reports were soon published on English, mathematics, science, and design and technology. The following intended timetable allowed for a brisk implementation over the early years of the 1990s. Note the 'key stages':

Key Stage 1 = 5–7 (Infant 1 + 2)
Key Stage 2 = 7/8–11 (Junior 3 to 6)
Key Stage 3 = 11/12–14 (Secondary 1 to 3)
Key Stage 4 = 14/15–16 (Secondary 4 and 5)

Table 4.1

| Academic year | | Maths and science | Technology | English |
|---|---|---|---|---|
| 1989–90 | Autumn 1989 | Attainment targets etc. for key stages 1 and 3 | | Attainment targets etc. for key stage 1 (probably) |
| 1990–91 | Autumn 1990 | Attainment targets etc. for key stage 2 | Attainment targets etc. for key stages 1–3 possibly (or 1 and 3) | Attainment targets etc for key stages 2 and 3 |
| | Summer 1991 | Unreported assessment for key stage 1 | | Unreported assessment for key stage 1 (probably) |
| 1991–92 | Autumn 1991 | | Attainment targets etc. for key stage 2 (possibly) | |
| | Summer 1992 | Reported assessment for key stage 1 Unreported assessment for key stage 3 | Unreported assessment for key stage 1 | Reported assessment for key stage 1 (probably) |
| 1992–93 | Autumn 1992 | Attainment targets etc. for key stage 4 | | Attainment targets etc. for key stage 4 |
| | Summer 1993 | Reported assessment for key stage 3 | Reported assessment for key stage 1 Unreported assessment for key stage 3 | Unreported assessment for key stage 3 |

| | | | | |
|---|---|---|---|---|
| **1993–94** | **Autumn 1993** | | Attainment targets for key stage 4 | |
| | **Summer 1994** | GCSEs for key stage 4<br>Unreported assessment for key stage 2 | Possibly, unreported assessment for key stage 2<br>Reported assessment for key stage 3 | Unreported assessment for key stage 2<br>Reported assessment for key stage 3<br>GCSEs for key stage 4 |
| **1994–95** | **Autumn 1994** | | | |
| | **Summer 1995** | Reported assessment for key stage 2 | Reported or unreported assessment for key stage 2 | Reported assessment for key stage 2 |
| **1995–96** | **Summer 1996** | | GCSEs for key stage 4<br>Possibly, reported assessment for key stage 2 | |

## Mathematics

Very quickly, before the Bill became an Act of Parliament, working parties were established in Core Subjects to prepare drafts of attainment targets, which in turn would determine the programmes of study. In each case, the reports would specify:

1. The knowledge, skills and understanding which pupils of different abilities and maturities are expected to have by the end of each key stage – the 'attainment targets';
2. The 'matters, skills, and processes' which are required to be taught to pupils of different abilities during each key stage – the 'programmes of study';
3. The arrangements for assessing the pupils for purposes of ascertaining what they have achieved in relation to the attainment targets.

The interim report in mathematics interpreted these requirements as follows. There are general principles. Thus there should be 'continuity and progression' from 5 to 16 in the main areas of mathematics. What is learned should also be practical and useful for solving everyday practical problems.

The main areas are 'number', 'algebra', 'measurement', 'space and shape', and 'handling data' (statistics and probability). By specifying attainment targets at ten different levels in each of these areas, you have a map of the mathematics curriculum 5 to 16 (Table 4.2).

However, for purpose of assessment, these attainment targets are placed in three (not five) *profile components*, one of which is concerned with the practical applications of mathematics (Table 4.3).

There are four programmes of study to help in the attainment of these targets. Programme A is intended for the infant phase and covers Levels 1 to 3 (i.e. the normal 7-year-old should reach Level 3). At this early stage, reference is made to the kind of qualities I picked out on page 32: basic skills, growing independence, problem-solving skills, patterning in shapes, matching, etc.

**Table 4.2**

| Level | Number | Algebra | Measures | Shape & Space | Data handling |
|---|---|---|---|---|---|
| 1 | Numbers to at least 10, addition and subtraction no greater than 10 | Repeating patterns | Length, weight and capacity comparisons | 3-D and 2-D shapes | Simple maps and diagrams |
| 2 | Numbers to at least 100, everyday fractions | Addition and subtraction up to 10 | Non-standard measures in length, capacity, weight and time | Everyday shapes such as squares, circles, spheres and triangles | Frequency tables and block graphs |
| 3 | Numbers to at least 1,000, decimal currency, multiplication up to 5×5 in 2, 5 and 10 | Division for 2, 5 and 10 | Metric calculation | Basic properties of 2-D and 3-D shapes, compass bearings | Information from tables and bar charts, simple computer data |
| 4 | Numbers of any size, multiplication up to 10×10 | Simple formulae, functions and inequalities expressed in writing | Scale in maps and drawings, area and volume | Construction of simple 2-D and 3-D shapes, measuring angles | Line graphs and interpretation of pie charts |

| | | | | |
|---|---|---|---|---|
| 5 | A range of fractions and percentages | Square roots, cubes and equations | Imperial units and their metric equivalents | Properties of intersecting and parallel lines and triangles | Frequency tables, conversion graphs, and flow diagrams |
| 6 | Conversion of fractions to decimals and percentages | Trial and exploration of different sequency patterns | Compound measures such as speed and density, converting metric units | Angle and symmetry properties of triangles etc. | Opinion and fact finding surveys based on yes/no answers |
| 7 | Memory facilities of a calculator, multiplication and division of any power of 10 | Complex number patterns | Recognition of degrees of error in measurement | Pythagoras' theorem | Specification and testing of a simple hypothesis |
| 8 | Calculation with fractions, index notation to represent powers and roots | Relationships between powers and roots, algebraic expression rules | Length, area and volume in calculation of plane and solid shapes | Sine, cosine, tangent and Pythagoras' theorem in 2-D contexts | Histograms, opinion surveys to elicit three or more answers to questions, calculation of probability |

**Tabel 4.2 continued**

| Level | Number | Algebra | Measures | Shape & Space | Data handling |
|---|---|---|---|---|---|
| 9 | Accurate addition, subtraction, division and multiplication, rational and irrational numbers | Interpretation of straight line law, quadratic equations and graphs | Surface area of cylinders and volumes of cones and spheres | Trigonometric ratios used in 3-D work | Presentation of complex data in simple and various graphs and diagrams |
| 10 | Calculation of the upper and lower bounds in subtraction, multiplication and division | How sequences merge using calculators and computers | Analysing error in calculations involving measurement | Angle properties of circles | Input and output diagrams |

*Education* (12 August 1988)

**Table 4.3**

| *Profile component 1* | *Profile component 2* | *Profile component 3* |
|---|---|---|
| Knowledge, skills and understanding in: <br> • numbers <br> • algebra <br> • measures | Knowledge, skills and understanding in: <br> • shape and space <br> • data handling | Practical application of mathematics |

Programme B is aimed at the junior phase and covers Levels 2 to 6 (note the overlap with the previous programme). At this stage, there is a consolidation of basic skills, but also a growing familiarity with calculators.

Programme C aims at ages 11 to 14 with Levels 4 to 8. Practical investigations are required; use should be made of computers.

Programme D is geared to ages 14 to 16 with levels 5 to 10, and should be looking outwards towards the world of work (including 'entrepreneurism'!). And all these programmes will include not only writing and reading, but also listening, talking, reflecting, practical work and drafting.

It should be said that this was an interim report, and much had to be done or agreed before the attainment targets and programmes of study became legally binding on all schools. Indeed, the process whereby this happens is an interesting one. The mathematics proposals are referred to the National Curriculum Council. The NCC then consults widely. Following consultation, it reports to the Secretary of State with recommendations. He or she then publishes a draft of the 'proposed order', followed by a period of at least one month of further consultation. After this, the Secretary makes it 'an order' which becomes legally binding. The Secretary of State, thereby, has full powers to determine the precise attainment targets of every child in the country.

## English

The English Working Party produced an interim report on 14 November 1988. This was only six months after it was appointed, which shows how quickly the details were being sketched of attainment targets and programmes of study within the Core Subjects of the National Curriculum. This report was confined to the primary stage – a report on the secondary stage was to be available six months later.

The report expressed its agreement with the underlying principle of the Kingman Report (see page 20), but went beyond it in taking on board not only English language but also English literature. Therefore, the following major principles are stated: first, that all pupils have an entitlement to learn standard English; secondly, that knowledge *about* English is important – about nouns, verbs, adjectives, etc. (the 'parts of speech'; there is no doubt that, with changing fashions in English teaching, many teachers do not see this to be important); thirdly, that children should be introduced to a wide range of literary forms, including books from the wider English-speaking world. (Note here the multiculturism: 'Children need to be aware of the richness of contemporary writing, so that they may be introduced to the ideas and feelings of people from cultures different from their own'.)

The report is still reticent about setting too limited a set of attainment objectives, and gives little cause for complaint in what it does 'prescribe'. There is a list of a couple of hundred authors whose work children should have access to but no prescribed texts. None the less, as in the mathematics and science reports, it requires the classification of different areas of attainment for five levels appropriate to the primary stage:

1. Speaking and Listening – one set of attainment targets.
2. Reading – two sets of attainment targets:
   (i) Reading and responding to writing;
   (ii) Information-retrieval strategies.
3. Writing – three sets of attainment targets:
   (i) Writing;

(ii) Spelling;
(iii) Handwriting.

To reach these attainment targets, there are prescribed 'programmes of study' – although these are put forward in such general terms that they permit considerable professional freedom to the teachers. For example, if you take the target area 'speaking and listening', the pupils should be able to:

*Level*    *Description*
1.    Speak freely, and listen, one-to-one to a peer-group member. Respond to simple classroom instructions given by a teacher.

2.    In a range of activities (including problem-solving), speak freely, and listen, to a small group of peers.

Listen attentively, and respond, to stories and poetry.

Speak freely to the teacher; listen and make verbal and non-verbal responses as appropriate.

Respond to an increasing range and complexity of classroom instructions.

3.    Present real or imaginary events in a connected narrative to a small group of peers, speaking freely and audibly.

Convey accurately a simple message.

Give and receive simple instructions and respond appropriately.

Listen attentively for increased periods of time and respond as appropriate.

4.    Describe an event or experience to a group of peers, clearly, audibly and in detail.

Give and receive precise instructions and follow them.

Ask relevant questions with increasing confidence.

Offer a reasoned explanation of how a task has been done or a problem has been solved.

Take part effectively in a small group discussion and respond to others in the group.

Make confident use of the telephone.

Speak freely and audibly to a class.

Speak freely and audibly to the adults encountered in school.

5. Speak freely and audibly to a larger audience of peers and adults.

Discuss and debate constructively, advocating and justifying a particular point of view.

Contribute effectively to a small group discussion which aims to reach agreement on a given assignment.

To attain these targets, the programme of study prescribed would enable the children 'to encounter an extensive range of materials, situations and activities planned to develop their capacity and confidence in talking and listening', by using role-play and drama. This 'encounter' would be quite purposeful, developing the 'children's grasp of sequence, cause and effect, reasoning, sense of consistency, appreciation of relevance and irrelevance and powers of prediction and recall'. For example, for pupils aged 5 to 7, the range of activities should include:

- casual talk;
- response to visual and aural stimuli;
- imaginative play and improvised drama;
- listening to well-chosen and well-read stories, rhymes, poems, plays and other writing;
- listening to and telling unscripted stories;
- sharing experiences (games in and out of school) with the teacher, other pupils and parents;
- asking and answering questions;
- giving and receiving simple explanations and information;
- giving and receiving simple instructions, with opportunities for appropriate response.

## Science

Remember that the Act specifies the need for attainment targets in each of the subjects at different ages, and defines these attainment targets as

> the knowledge, skills and understanding which pupils of different abilities and maturities are expected to have by the end of each key stage

and defines programmes of study as

> the matters, skills and processes which are required to be taught to pupils of different abilities during each key stage.

The working group reported in August 1988. It recommended 22 attainment targets for students aged 11 to 16, only 17 of which it deemed suitable for pupils aged 7 to 11. These attainment targets were:

1. (1)   The variety of life
   (2)   Processes of life
   (3)   Genetics and evolution
   (4)   Human influences on the earth
   (5)   Types and uses of materials
   (6)   Making new materials (not for 5 to 11)
   (7)   Explaining how materials behave (not for 5 to 11)
   (8)   Earth and atmosphere
   (9)   Forces
   (10) Electricity and magnetism
   (11) Information transfer
   (12) Energy transfer
   (13) Energy resources (not for 5 to 11)
   (14) Sound and music
   (15) Using light
   (16) The Earth in space
2. (17) Exploration and investigation: doing
   (18) Exploration and investigation: working in group
3. (19) Communication: reporting and responding
   (20) Communication: using secondary sources

4. (21) Science in action: technological and social aspects (not for 5 to 11)

   (22) Science in action: the nature of science (not for 5 to 11)

Each of these attainment targets is then translated into statements of attainment at each of the ten levels. For example in Attainment Target 1, the variety of life, the statements of attainment are that pupils should:

*Level*

1.  Know about the wide variety of living things, which includes human beings.

2.  Know about the conditions that plants and animals need for life.

    Know about handling living things with care and confidence.

3.  Be able to recognise similarities and differences among living things.

    Be able to sort living things into broad groups according to observable features.

    Know that living things respond to seasonal and daily changes.

4.  Be able to recognise similarities and differences both within and between groups of plants and animals.

    Know that different organisms live in different places and feed on different things.

    Know about decay and the re-use of biological material.

5.  Understand that the differences in physical factors between localities are reflected in the different species of plants and animals found there.

    Be able to assign organisms to their major groups using keys and observable features.

Know why fertilisers are used in agriculture and horticulture.

6. Understand that organisms have features which enable them to survive in the conditions where they normally live.

   Know about how human well-being can be influenced by environmental factors.

7. Know that the balance of materials in a biological community can be maintained by the recycling of materials and that human activities can affect this recycling.

   Know about feeding relationships and the pyramid of numbers in biological communities.

8. Understand the cycling of an important element, including the role of microbes and other living things in maintaining the cycle.

   Know about the role of microbes in sewage disposal and composting.

   Understand pyramids of numbers and biomass and how materials for growth and energy are transferred through ecosystems.

9. Understand the relationships between population growth and decline and environmental resources, including the control of human populations.

   Understand that food production involves the manipulation of ecosystems or the creation of artificial ecosystems.

10. Understand the cycling of the major elements (carbon, nitrogen, oxygen) and the role of microbes and other organisms in maintaining the cycles.

    Understand predator–prey relationships.

The programme of study supporting these attainment targets is:

5 to 7   Children should have opportunities to observe firsthand a variety of animal and plant life over a period of time in which they take responsibility for the care of these living things.

7 to 11   Children should explore and investigate a range of different localities and the ways in which plants and animals are suited to their location (8). They should explore the ways in which plant and animal behaviour and life cycles are influenced by seasonal and daily changes (2, 8, 16).

They should have the opportunity to develop skills in identifying locally occurring species of plants and animals by using observable structural features of organisms (2, 3).

11 to 14   Pupils should study a variety of localities at first hand, or through secondary sources, to investigate the range of seasonal and daily variability in physical factors and the features of organisms which enable them to survive these changes (2).

They should relate environmental factors to human well-being (2, 14).

They should explore, in a general way, the cycling of materials made possible by the activity of microbes and other living organisms.

They should broaden their study of locally occurring plants and animals to other organisms and, through this, be introduced to the major taxonomic groups (2). They should have opportunities to group organisms on the basis of similarities and differences and to use keys to name organisms.

14 to 16   Pupils should make a more detailed and quantitative study of a locality, including the investigation of the abundance and distribution of common species, and the ways in which they are adapted to

their location (4). They should explore the factors affecting population size, including human populations.

They should consider the cycling of elements and the impact of human activity on these cycles in managed ecosystems like farms and forests (8).

The working party judged that it would be necessary for science to occupy about 20 per cent of the curriculum time.

## Design and technology

The Technology Working Group first reported in November 1988. It had only been set up on 29 April and that shows the speed with which the establishment of the National Curriculum progressed. The report called for a rationalisation of the several subjects that are technologically based so that there could be a 'well planned, steady progress' from 5 to 16. The Group paid particular attention to overcoming gender differences in expectation and attainment.

I wish to spend a greater proportion of space on this 'Foundation Subject' because it illustrates very powerfully both the possibilities and the difficulties in the Foundation Subject approach to a National Curriculum. First, design and technology does, as with English, deal with an activity that goes 'across the curriculum, drawing on and linking with a wide range of subjects' – it involves the pupils making judgements of many kinds: technical, economic, social, aesthetic, etc. None the less, it represents something distinctive – the purposeful and practical response to 'perceived needs or opportunities' that must be worked out in particular contexts and against the background of particular values. It is about being practically but intelligently 'capable' – of doing, of making, of 'knowing how'. It cannot, therefore, be approached merely from books. Nor can its success be assessed in terms of the written word, as opposed to the activity. Design and technology is about intelligent activity that might have several possible outcomes and that draws upon several different subjects.

Secondly, it is assumed, in the report, that many of the experiences and activities within the primary and secondary schools already contribute to the aims of design and technology. None the less, what is necessary is a more systematic approach – developmentally (i.e. ensuring that there is progress in the acquisition of appropriate knowledge, capabilities and attitudes) and organisationally (i.e. ensuring that there is no unnecessary overlap from one part of the curriculum to another, or that one design and technology-type activity reinforces another).

Thirdly, however, such a wide-ranging concept of design and technology can create problems of sorting out the distinctive contribution of the several subjects which are not mentioned in the National Curriculum but which might be seen to make a contribution to design and technology – indeed, must do if they are to survive. I am thinking of home economics, business studies, computer studies, and craft, design and technology.

To this end, the report established five attainment targets:

1. Exploration and investigation of contexts for design and technological activities;
2. Formulation of proposals, and choice of design for, development;
3. Development of the design and plan for the making of an artefact or system;
4. Making of artefacts and systems;
5. Appraisal of the processes, outcomes and effects of design and technological activities.

There is only one 'profile component' for all of this – that is, only one general category of what one is seeking to achieve, namely, a general capability to carry through the whole process 1 to 5. Knowledge alone is insufficient. To be capable (which, of course, requires knowledge) is all important.

The attainment targets are:

*Attainment target 1:* Through exploration and investigation of a range of contexts (personal, social, environmental, business, industrial), pupils should be able to identify and state clearly needs and opportunities for design and technological activities.

*Attainment target 2:* Pupils should be able to explore, develop and combine design and technological proposals, and use their judgements, based on various criteria (economic, technical, aesthetic, ergonomic, environmental, social) to choose an appropriate design for further development.

*Attainment target 3:* Pupils should be able to develop their chosen design by refining and adding detail, and to produce a plan for making the required artefact or system by identifying tasks and sub-tasks, and ways of undertaking them, and by making judgements of what is realistic, appropriate and achievable.

*Attainment target 4:* Working to a scheme derived from their previously developed design, pupils should be able to identify, manage and use appropriate resources, including both knowledge and processes, in order to make an artefact or system.

*Attainment target 5:* Pupils should be able to produce a critical appraisal of the processes, outcomes and effects of their own design and technological activity, as well as of the outcomes and effects of the design and technological activity of others, both historic and present day. With respect to their own activity, they should be able to use their appraisal to propose and justify modifications to the processes they have used and to the outcomes realised.

An example of the statements of attainment for Target 4 is shown in Table 4.4.

The interim report is a well-written and thoughtful document. It captures the cross-curriculum significance of design and technology. It stresses the practical knowledge and capability – which is academically and intellectually just as demanding as 'traditional learning'. It in no way shirks, however, the significance of knowledge in the sense of concepts to be acquired and facts to be learnt. It is not *just* a matter of

**Table 4.4: Attainment Target 4**

*STATEMENTS OF ATTAINMENT*

| *Level 4 (average 11-year-old), pupils should be able to:* | *Level 5/6 (average 14-year-old), pupils should be able to:* |
|---|---|
| 1. use hand tools and simple equipment appropriate to the materials to be worked, safely and with a broad degree of accuracy (for example, use scissors to cut cardboard, a saw to cut wood, a computer keyboard to enter data); | 1. use a range of hand and powered tools and equipment (for example, plane, airbrush, cooker, database and spreadsheet software package, sewing-machine) with due regard to function, safety and the need to leave them in a fit condition for future use; |
| | 2. prepare tools and equipment for use (for example, checking routines for powered tools and equipment, setting tension on a sewing-machine, setting for depth of cut); |
| | 3. use these tools and equipment to a level of precision and finish appropriate to the working characteristics of the materials and the function of the artefact or system, justifying any departure from the design brief (for example, setting in hinges to a box lid, inserting a concealed zip); |
| 2. use under supervision making and assembling procedures appropriate to the range of tools and materials; | 4. use an increased range of making and assembling procedures required by the range of tools and materials, including techniques such as preparing and marking out timber, preparing and cutting out a fabric to a pattern, and assembling several components |

| Level 4 (continued) | Level 5/6 (continued) |
|---|---|
| | (for example, an electrical circuit, using a spreadsheet and database together in an IT system); |
| 3. use simple plans, drawings and diagrams to assist making (for example, use their working sketches and diagrams to make a vehicle which moves); | 5. interpret plans, drawings and diagrams (for example a switching circuit, a working drawing, a dress pattern) in order to achieve the outcome described; |
| 4. suggest a possible solution to a problem which arises during making (for example, suggest different means of dealing with wheel spin in a vehicle they have designed). | 6. alter planned procedures to cope with unforeseen problems arising from the materials or tools being used (for example, power failure, component breakage). |

process. None the less, one can foresee very real problems. First, some of the attainment targets will be reached through other areas of the curriculum – not necessarily called design and technology. Hence, it will be necessary *organisationally* to think across the curriculum, not to identify the Foundation Subject 'Design and Technology' with a subject in the sense of a separate space on the timetable. Secondly, it will be 'delivered' through a range of subjects which have played an important part in the school curriculum but which get no mention in the Education Act. Take home economics, for example. This subject is very important: it provides an active learning environment for the students which they appreciate; it bridges the divide between the academic and the personal and social development; it introduces the students to an area that is seen to be 'relevant' while at the same time demanding a disciplined, technical and scientific approach to problems. If design and technology is to be delivered partly through home economics, then one of two things could happen unless one is careful. Either home economics loses its distinctive character

– the particular contribution it has made to personal and social education and to linking school with community; or it may disappear altogether, for if it is but one possible way of teaching design and technology, then it may easily be seen as a poor substitute for craft, design and technology or computer studies, which may be seen to illustrate the processes more effectively.

## Assessment within the National Curriculum

Assessment arrangements are integral to curriculum design.

The reason is quite simple. Work has to be matched to the level of attainment of the young learner. It is no good giving work to pupils which is far too difficult for them to understand. A fuller account of testing and assessment issues arising from the 1988 Act can be found in another book in this series, *Testing and Assessment*, by Charles Desforges.

There are several different, though related, functions for assessment:

1. to find out what children know or can do, with a view to planning one's teaching;
2. to find out why children cannot do something or do not understand (diagnostic);
3. to find out whether one has been teaching successfully;
4. to provide information in order to compare performances:
   - between different stages of a child's life,
   - between children,
   - between schools.

Different sorts of assessment are necessary for different functions. Thus, an assessment may tell you that the children have not learnt anything, but it may not help you to diagnose the problem. Also, there are dangers in using tests that let you know what children have learnt, as the basis of comparisons. Different schools may have been highlighting different objectives. None the less, assessment of some sort is essential and teachers are doing it all the time. It is important, therefore, to be systematic about it – to make sure the assessments tie in closely with the curriculum objectives and to make sure that there is a suitable way of conveying the results.

In anticipation of the 1988 Education Act, a Task Group on Assessment and Testing (TGAT) was formed to explore how children's progress across the subjects of the National Curriculum might be assessed. The Task Group reported in 1988.

The system proposed is both 'formative' and 'summative'. That is, it is intended both to help teachers teach more effectively and to provide, at 16, a summation of what the young person knows and can do. This has, of course, implications for the GCSE because it would seem foolish to assess young people twice in each subject at the age of 16 – once through GCSE and the other on Foundation Subject performance. Some commentators saw this development as signalling the end of the GCSE.

Not only must it tie in with the GCSE, however, it must also link somehow with the Recording of Achievement (see page 24). Perhaps the Foundation Subject assessments will constitute the academic part of a much broader profile.

One important feature of the new proposals, implicit in the details I have already given of the suggested attainment targets in four subjects, is that the tests will be criterion-referenced, not norm-referenced: that is, the tests will reveal what the student knows or can do. It measures performance against a set of statements or criteria of satisfactory performance. This is different from norm-references testing which simply says how someone stands in relation to other 'performers'.

As we said in connection with the interim subject reports, there are several key features of the assessment arrangements for the National Curriculum.

1. The identification within each subject of attainment targets in terms of knowledge, understanding and skills.

2. The clustering of these attainment targets into four, five or six sub-divisions of the subject or 'profile components' (e.g. in science: exploration and investigation, communication, knowledge and understanding, science in action).

3. The identification across these clusterings of cross-curricular themes.

4. The translation of these attainment targets within each 'profile component' into statements of what children can or should do at ten different levels (NB These levels represent developmental 'stages' from 5 to 16, so that two children at different ages may have the same statements attributed to their separate performances – the performance of an 11-year-old may be described in exactly the same way as the performance of a 14-year-old). Each level represents the average educational progress of a child over about two years. This can be shown diagrammatically, as in Figure 4.1.

Hence, we would expect 7-year-olds to have the attainment targets specified at Levels 1 to 3, 11-year-olds those specified at Levels 3 to 5, 14-year-olds those specified at Levels 4 to 8, and 16-year-olds those specified at 5 to 10.

5. The devising of national tests to assess the level of attainment and of teacher 'home-based' assessments to supplement

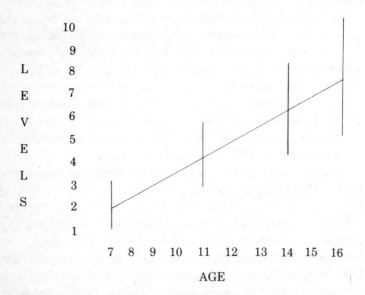

**Figure 4.1**

the tests. Such tests will need to go beyond traditional 'paper and pencil' tests because very often we want to report upon the practical ability or group work, something that cannot be tested by two-hour written examinations.

6. The reports of these assessments (the teachers' and the externally set ones) will need to be moderated before they become public knowledge.

7. Reports will give to parents the information about the different levels of performance, subject by subject, reached by their children – with comparative data on the other children in the school and nationally.

8. The reports will also be made more widely available, but 'only as part of a more general statement about the school, produced by the school and authenticated by the local education authority'.

9. Exemptions are permitted from these assessment arrangements on account of special educational needs.

There are anxieties about this aspect of the 1988 Education Reform Act.

First, assessment of many of the attainment targets requires a much more complex and generous approach to testing than resources might permit. To assess practical work requires, for instance, the presence of an observer on a one-to-one basis. Therefore, the tasks will be expensive to administer. The inability to provide this level of funding might mean that, to get them on the cheap, assessments are reduced to paper-and-pencil tests.

Secondly, the reports based on assessment according to criteria will give the very labels 'about ingredients' required by the consumer for informed choice between schools in the 'open market'. Supermarkets have their baked beans properly labelled for the discerning shopper, so too will schools: the ingredients being the educational performance on national tests of the children.

Thirdly, comparative figures on the results of the tests may well arise from comparing unlike with unlike. School X, despite its poorer results when compared with Y, may actually have performed better because X has a more difficult group of young people to deal with. At a time of 'open admissions', reports, misinterpreted, could cause much damage. And people may not be satisfied with the gloss that LEAs will be giving to explain away the otherwise poor results. People tend not to read the gloss, only the figures.

Thus School X in a very poor part of town might obtain an average score of Level 4 for its 11-year-olds. School Y in a wealthy and privileged suburb of the same town might obtain an average of 4.5. The 'league table' would see School Y as being above School X. In reality, School X might be a superb school whose pupils scored at Level 4 when other schools in similar circumstances only scored at Level 3. On the other hand, School Y, with its average of 4.5, might be below the Level 5 average of other schools in equally privileged circumstances. Test scores of individual pupils, classes or schools must be interpreted with intelligence and sensitivity to the many factors influencing them.

# Chapter 5

# GETTING THE ACT TOGETHER

The curriculum is the planned way in which we help children to learn. Therefore, it will state the kind of things that need to be learnt – the skills and knowledge and understandings in mathematics, say, or in English. It should also say something about *how* the students are to learn – the approaches to learning and the way in which it is to be organised. The reason for that is simple. Children can learn as much from *how* something is put across as from the *content* of the lesson itself. If you want to teach the importance of poetry, then it must be presented in a manner that demonstrates that importance. If religious education is taught by someone ignorant of or indifferent to the subject – the last period on Friday – then, even if the syllabus is covered, the message is loud and clear. The children would have learnt that RE is unimportant – indeed, a trivial pursuit.

To plan a curriculum, therefore, you need to go back to more basic principles. What are the skills and knowledge which you value so much that you want the next generation of children to acquire – indeed, for which you are prepared to make them attend school from the age of 5 to that of 16, often against their will?

One major criticism of the 1988 Education Reform Act is that this sort of question was not addressed. The moral context of education received little more than cursory attention at the consultation stage, despite the fact that the personal development of young people is possibly the most important moral question that society needs to deal with.

I shall, therefore, say something about these broader educational principles before re-examining the National Curriculum to see what has been left out and what needs to be done.

## The educated person and educational traditions

'Education' is, of course, concerned with giving people knowledge. It is opposed to 'ignorance' – that failure to understand
or to see what is the case. But not any old knowledge will do.
I could devote all my life to studying the pebbles on Budleigh
Salterton beach. I would have an enormous amount of knowledge. Indeed, I would become the world's expert on that subject. But such a narrow focus would leave me woefully ignorant
of other important matters. I am sure that friends would recognise my vast knowledge on such a narrow subject, but would
not hold me up as the exemplar of an educated person.

Education, therefore, is concerned with helping people to
think and to understand. It is about *empowering* them – giving
them the mental tools to reflect, to reason, to argue and to
solve problems. It is about developing those human endow-
ments, those human qualities, whereby they can understand
themselves, other people and the world around them, and
therefore assume some measure of control over their own life
and destiny. It is not just a matter of acquiring knowledge; it
is a matter of acquiring understanding and insight. It is not
just a matter of being insightful in any old thing; it is a matter
of having insight into matters of importance. And it is not just
a matter of insight as such; it is a matter of being able to
translate those insights into meaningful courses of action.

The educated person – what we hope 'to produce' as a result
of our school curriculum – is, therefore, endowed with the
capacity to reason and to reflect, has a range of knowledge,
understandings and skills which we consider to be important,
and has the capability of translating this knowledge into practice. The educated person, thus armed, takes responsibility for
his or her own life, not in an arbitrary fashion, not in a state
of ignorance, but mentally and morally prepared for such a
task.

Therefore, the education of young children is a rather fear-
some responsibility. The educator (and the educational system
through which he or she works) must have a clear idea of
what is valuable to transmit – what kinds of knowledge and

understanding do empower the young person; what kind of contribution to society he should be equipped to make; what activities will help him to have the *capability* of acting autonomously but responsibly within that society. Education is necessarily shot through with values – the social values that we, as educators, are wanting to pass on, and the personal values that we are concerned to promote in each individual. Values are at the heart of the enterprise.

Implicit in the earlier part of this book are three quite distinct educational traditions competing for the overall direction of the curriculum. First, there is that tradition which sees the educated person to be one who has been initiated into the forms of knowledge that are represented by long-established subjects. Education is about knowledge and understanding; there are different kinds of knowledge and understanding; by learning the content of different subjects, you thus become knowledgeable in a broad and a balanced way. Moreover, these subjects represent the kinds of knowledge that do empower a young person to think, reflect and reason. The curriculum is essentially subject-based; the content of the curriculum is essentially taken from the traditional subjects.

A quite distinct tradition has a different starting-point, and we saw this with certain aspects of the pre-vocational curriculum represented by TVEI. There it is not taken for granted that personal qualities – such as understanding other people or the practicalities of life, assuming responsibility for one's own destiny, being capable of tackling practical or personal problems – are acquired from learning the different subjects in a broad and balanced curriculum. Of course, what subjects represent is important. Of course, young people need to learn the knowledge and concepts in science and mathematics and history. But they need much more than that in their personal lives. And, moreover, the value of these subjects, the value of the knowledge that they contain depends on what value the child finds in it to help him or her live a fulfilled and satisfying life. Is it valuable to learn mathematics until 16, when all the child needs to know for practical purposes has been learnt by the age of 11? Is it not much more important to learn such personal and social qualities as team work, co-operation, the capacity to communicate effectively to different types of people, the confidence to tackle unexpected problems, the moral strength to face life when it gets tough, the practical knowledge required to survive in everyday life, the enterprise required to survive in business? And none of these might be acquired through learning history or geography. This tradition, therefore, starts not with subjects, but with what it means to be, to grow, and to be effective as a person.

We have also seen that there is a third competing tradition, namely, that of the useful curriculum – one that produces the knowledge, the skills and the attitudes necessary for the world of work. A fully fledged 'useful curriculum' would not necessarily be balanced in the same way that the subject-based curriculum would be. The curriculum planning would start from a different place. It would ask what are the skills and knowledge required by society if job vacancies are to be filled and if future manpower planning targets are going to be met. The curriculum would aim to make sure that students had the appropriate attitudes towards business and industry, as well as the necessary vocational skills – entrepreneurial spirit and know-how, economic awareness of the wealth-producing sectors of society, and so on.

Of course, the curriculum could be an integration or an amalgam of all three traditions – a balance between subjects, vocationally oriented activities, such as work experience, and personally negotiated learning objectives, giving a different meaning to the concept of 'balance' as the one described on page 24. But the National Curriculum does not address itself to this problem. There is little to be said about the values that the curriculum should serve, and thus about the balance between subjects, personal relevance and social utility. In that, the National Curriculum ignores so much curriculum development that has emerged in schools in the last ten years as the teachers' response to the criticisms summarised on page 5.

Some of the most important omissions and areas of concern are discussed below.

## Areas of concern

### *Pre-vocational education*

It was explained in Chapter 2 how significant had been the Technical and Vocational Education Initiative (TVEI). It is significant, however, that this initiative emerged not from the DES but from the Department of Employment, via the Manpower Services Commission. Announced in November 1982, in rather narrow vocational terms, it was transformed by teachers into a radical challenge to traditional ways in which we think about and plan the curriculum. It had a vocational orientation, certainly. It was, and is, concerned about the personal and social qualities, and the basic skills, which are necessary for young people if they are to be effective and responsible as adults, especially in the world of work. But it drew much of its philosophy and values from the person-centred tradition referred to above. Central to many of the TVEI schemes, and to the similar courses which schools were adopting from the City and Guilds of London Institute and from the Business and Technician Education Council, was the aim of empowering young people to take responsibility for their own learning – through the negotiation of learning objectives, through a much greater stress upon practical learning, through finding a place for *their* experience at the centre of the curriculum, through a system of guidance and counselling whereby they could make better sense of *their* futures, and so on. The curriculum practices that emerged from such aims did indeed transform the educational experience of many young people. Exeter University School of Education has interviewed nearly 2,000 young people in the last five years about their experience of TVEI, and the enthusiastic welcome given to the different mode of learning and to the different content has been unmistakable, even from those who otherwise were alienated from a curriculum which did not seem relevant to them.

And yet, in the consultation document that preceded the National Curriculum, only two brief and grudging references were made to TVEI, and in no way did that experience seem to influence the legislation. It is a question of lessons not learnt from a £1 billion investment.

### The world of work

One major criticism of schools had been that they had not prepared students adequately for the world of work. This is not an easy criticism to understand. Certainly those firmly embedded within the subject-based tradition would reject that that is the function of schools, except in the very general sense of producing broadly educated people who *thereby* are better prepared to learn the skills and knowledge for specific jobs.

It is argued, however, that preparation for the world of work has to be much more direct than that. Employers complain not just about the lack of basic skills – of literacy and of numeracy – but about the inappropriate attitudes towards industry and commerce. There seems to be an anti-industrial spirit deeply rooted in our culture.

To meet that criticism, schools have responded remarkably quickly. Most young people will enjoy some work-experience before they are 16. Many will engage in mini-enterprise schemes in which they simulate or even participate in small businesses. Schools have established links with industry. I know of one where the pupils research, write and produce a high-quality newsletter for a local business; another school nearby manufactures board games in French which the students sell in a Brittany market.

Indeed, schools–industry links have been part of a major initiative in January 1988, from the Department of Trade and Industry (DTI), called the 'Enterprise and Education Initiative'. This has three major objectives. First, to find places in industry for 10 per cent of all teachers in any one year; secondly, to ensure work-experience of at least two weeks for all young people before they leave school; thirdly, to ensure that all future teachers receive adequate preparation for this during their initial training. There are, needless to say, daft aspects of this policy. When asked about the capacity of industry to absorb 50,000 teachers and 600,000 students per year and to give them a worthwhile educational experience on top of the provision of 400,000 YTS places, a spokesman from the DTI could give me no satisfactory answer. The significance for my argument, however, is that, however foolishly it is carried out in practice, there have been immense strides forward in exploring and implementing links between schools and industry in order to give the curriculum a greater vocational orientation – with particular emphasis upon fostering the appropriate attitudes towards this aspect of adult life. When the National Curriculum was first announced, however, it was as though these developments had not taken place.

Three major departments of State now have a stake in the curriculum – the DES, the Department of Employment and the DTI. It is confusing to teachers and parents alike when schools are expected to respond to all three departments and yet when the National Curriculum, established by one, ignored the initiatives of the two others. The successful implementation of the National Curriculum will certainly require all three government departments to collaborate effectively with schools and local authorities.

## Personal and social education

Much of the time, energy and curriculum thinking of teachers are devoted to the personal and social development of young people: equipping them with the inter-personal skills and with the qualities that help them to function effectively and responsibly inside and outside the school. A great deal of this, of course, is achieved through the kinds of relationships that are established between teacher and pupil. The general ethos or atmosphere of the school is all important.

None the less, there has been a great deal of curriculum thinking in this area, too – the systematic planning of activities with personal and social development in mind. Two very significant curriculum developments were the Developmental

Group Work of Leslie Button and the closely connected Active Tutorial Work of Baldwin and Wells. But there are many other schemes, as well. Indeed, the centrality of drama in the experience of young people is partly justified on these grounds. The tutorial work, the drama, the personal guidance, the negotiation of learning objectives, are all geared to developing the trust, the confidence, the ideals, the imagination and empathy, the sense of responsibility, and the autonomy which are crucial to personal and social development of young people. These must have a place in curriculum design and planning. They receive hardly a mention in the National Curriculum.

There are specific aspects of this – for example, health education. The work of John Balding at Exeter University School of Education shows the school-based enquiry that might effectively provide the base for a home-grown curriculum, highly relevant to the personal needs of the young people. Each year thousands of pupils fill in a health-related behaviour questionnaire which is analysed at Exeter University. Teachers can then see what health issues they need to address in their own school. For example, they may discover that boys do not clean their teeth regularly, though girls do, or that teenage drinking is a problem, or that many pupils who smoke would like to give it up. Indeed, there has been a lot of investment in this curriculum 'subject'. But health educators, often part of the personal and social education team, are rightly concerned that as such it seems to have little place in the National Curriculum, which begins from a list of subjects rather than from an analysis of personal and social needs.

### Areas of controversy

A dilemma that many teachers have to face daily is that of teaching about issues which are highly charged with controversy and yet about which young people need to be informed. The dilemma is this: to prepare young people for the future they have to accept responsibility for political and moral decisions which, one hopes, will be based on reflection, reason and considered judgement. They often seek guidance and counselling. And yet the teachers may feel that professionally they are not able to promote one set of values rather than another, or one political position rather than another, since there is no consensus in our society on such matters. For example, parents or members of the public may feel that teachers have gone beyond their professional responsibilities if they promote CND or anti-nuclear solutions to our energy problems; others, by the same token, may feel equally enraged if teachers used the classroom to promote 'Peace through NATO'. The question is: should the teacher use his or her authority to promote a particular set of political beliefs or values? It would seem wrong for the teacher to do so, and yet political education would seem essential to any preparation for living in a democracy.

Another example would be in moral education, more specifically in sex education. Every school is obliged, following the 1986 Education Act, to have a policy on sex education, approved by the governors. It is also obliged by the same Act to give a balanced view of politically contentious issues. There are, however, various moral stances towards sexual relations which responsible adults take within our society – concerning homosexual relations, concerning sexual relationships outside marriage, concerning the prevention or termination of pregnancies. The promotion of one set of beliefs will offend those groups that hold the opposite beliefs. And there seems no clear and objective way of solving the differences. This is an example of controversial issues which have to be dealt with by the teacher but about which there seems to be no clear way forward. The handling of political and moral issues was omitted from early discussions about the National Curriculum. But controversial issues cannot be avoided by adults in their daily lives and there are frequently documentaries on them on radio and television. On the other hand, how to handle contentious matters is not clear. It is something that needs to be addressed by teachers in co-operation with parents and with the governing bodies.

## Religious education

Religious education is a controversial area in that, as with political and moral education, it deals with issues about which there is little consensus. Indeed, many do not have religious beliefs – or, if they do, attach little interest or value to them. But religious education has a unique place because its teaching is obligatory under the 1944 Education Act, and it does receive specific mention in the 1988 Education Reform Act.

Indeed, when the Bill was debated in the House of Lords, the teaching of RE was the central issue. Why? It is not a Foundation Subject, constrained within nationally established attainment targets and assessments. It is, however, a basic subject – a compulsory part of the curriculum though locally devised in accordance with agreed syllabuses or denominational interests in the voluntary aided and maintained schools.

RE is a subject where there has been much exciting development over the past few years. Teachers have endeavoured to avoid the 'confessional approach' – that is a conception of RE teaching which is directed at confirming the faith or converting. Instead, it has aimed at understanding and at appreciating the underlying significance and spirituality represented by RE. It is felt, however, that, as a result of the 1988 Education Reform Act and of the amendments in the House of Lords, there is a return to a more confessional approach. Indeed, Christianity is expressly mentioned in legislation for the first time.

The reality, however, is a little different from what is popularly believed. First, there are Standing Advisory Councils on RE (SACRE) which have the job of reviewing agreed syllabuses and of advising LEAs. Membership of the SACRE must include 'such Christian and other religious denominations as, in the opinion of the [local] authority, will appropriately reflect the principal religious traditions in the area'. It is the case that new RE syllabuses must 'reflect the fact that the religious traditions in Great Britain are in the main Christian whilst taking account of the teaching and practices of the other principal religions represented in Great Britain', but this does not entail that Christianity should be *promoted* or even constitute a central feature of religious teaching.

In addition, daily acts of collective worship are also sustained, the majority of which in each term must be 'wholly or mainly of a broadly Christian character', though not distinctive of any one Christian denomination. Of course, parents retain the right to remove their children. And in special cases (where, for instance, a school has a largely Muslim population) the head can seek permission of the local SACRE to have the requirement of such an act of worship changed.

### Special educational needs

One widespread anxiety over the Act was its failure to take into account the requirements of children with special educational needs, despite the considerable thought and recommendation devoted to this area by the Warnock Report (see page 18) and subsequent legislation. The problems are these. First, appropriate education of young people with special learning difficulties requires a curriculum more tailor-made to those needs. It must arise from proper diagnosis. That will entail a more individualised approach to the curriculum than is envisaged in the Education Reform Act. And remember that, according to Warnock, roughly 20 per cent of the school population could be said at some time to fall into this category. Setting norms of attainment for the population as a whole, therefore, has been seen by many not to take sufficient account of the individual variation – both in learning problems and in rates of growth. It has always been a hallmark of the professional teacher that he or she can match the curriculum to the individual needs.

Secondly, and possibly more significantly, the tying of a national assessment system to these norms could so easily militate against the interests of those young people whose needs are greatest. Imagine the scenario at a time of open admissions. Parents choose the school with 'the best record'. The best record will, in their eyes, be largely determined by the publicised results on the national attainment tests. It could easily be seen to be to a school's advantage to exclude those young people with special needs whose scores will no doubt deflate the tested performance of that school. After all, in a market economy with freedom of choice, one does tend to read the labels before purchase. The tinkering about with the Bill during its passage through Parliament did not really affect these fundamental problems.

### The arts

The National Curriculum specifies music and art, and this has aggrieved those who have a wider interest in the arts than that. One is thinking particularly of drama and of dance. It is not clear how far this should be seen as a problem, except in terms of status that is given thereby to certain art forms rather than others. Drama could be incorporated into English; room could be found in the general arrangements for the arts (explicitly concerned only with music and art) for dance or drama; and there is some 20 per cent of time still supposedly spare outside the National Curriculum. But the problems are more basic than that because, in order to have good drama and dance, one needs the appropriately qualified staff employed on a full-time basis. It is difficult to see how that can be maintained after they have been evacuated from the National Curriculum.

### Cross-curriculum themes

As these and other points were put to Ministers after the publication of the Bill, the regular response was: 'cross-curriculum themes'. Economic awareness, enterprise, personal and social education, information technology, business studies, home economics, health education, and so on would be 'themes' either integrated into parts of the National Curriculum or taught across the curriculum. Thus home economics becomes part of design and technology. Information technology becomes a tool (like reading or writing) which facilitates learning in every subject. Economic awareness and enterprise become the background for teaching geography or history (think of those enterprising Elizabethan merchants who captured Philip II's gold). Health education is carved up into elements which find their places in science, in RE or in English.

This is not the best form of curriculum planning. It is curriculum 'on the hoof', the realisation that not all can be made to fit the pattern of the National Curriculum. Cross-curriculum themes must be listed, and judgements need to be made about how they can be accommodated in the National Curriculum programmes of study – a major challenge to the teacher.

## Assessment

Professor Charles Desforges has produced a separate book in this series on assessment, and therefore I shall not enter into that area in any detail. But assessment is the key element in the National Curriculum proposals – the checking in a public form of the attainment of children at 7, 11, 14 and 16 against nationally defined criteria. Perhaps this, above all, has created the anxiety and evoked the criticisms that have surrounded the Act.

The reason is twofold. First, the experience of assessment (think back to the days of the 11+) is that it tends to narrow rather than to broaden the educational experience of young people. Teachers, quite understandably, tend to teach to the tests, for success in such tests can make so much difference to the resourcing of the school and to the attraction provided for potential clients. Secondly, it is not easy to conceive of a national testing system that, to be economical, will not be confined to the cheaper forms of testing. When the Task Group on Assessment and Testing first reported in 1988 (see page 93), teachers were greatly relieved to see a broadly conceived form of testing envisaged – not just paper-and-pencil tests, but ones that involved the observation and reporting by teachers, the internal evaluation of the processes of learning or of doing as well as the external assessment of the product of that learning. Thus, for example, in design and technology the *process* of identifying a problem, thinking of alternative solutions, organising the materials, and devising tests for the finished product, is the key feature that needs to be assessed. And that can only be done through close moderation of the work as it is being designed and tested.

However, this generous view of assessment, though promoted by TGAT and the interim reports of the four working groups, needs proper government support, otherwise the temptation to settle for tests which involve the minimum of time to administer and score becomes overwhelming.

## Teachers

No amount of central direction can compensate for poor professional work in the classroom. The teacher is the key figure in any educational system. Alienate the teacher, and all good intentions come to nought. The good teacher needs to have his or her professionalism recognised and respected. That professionalism is rooted in the knowledge of the subject matter being taught, in the knowledge of how to put it across to children and encourage them to learn, and in the relationship established with children at school. Without an adequate supply and an adequate training of these teachers, no central prescriptions, however cleverly devised, can be implemented.

Many teachers welcomed broad guide-lines within which to work. They, too, wanted the continuity between stages of education, and the National Curriculum would provide the framework for that continuity. But there is a danger in too much prescription. Education is, as was explained at the beginning of this chapter, a matter of empowering children to think, to reflect, to reason, to argue, to question, to respond intelligently to difficulties. It takes place in the main in an educational atmosphere – and between people who share those very values. If teachers are to educate rather than merely to train, if they are to create the appropriate context for rational and reflective thinking to take place, then they too must be able to exercise those same values in the execution of their duties. Society cannot have effective education in a context that militates against the participation of teachers in the intel-

ligent planning of education for their children. Too much prescription from the centre would not allow for the educational
aims of the National Curriculum to be reached. There are
logical limits to the degree of detail that can be prescribed. The
National Curriculum can only work if central prescriptions
are intelligent, intelligible and capable of securing the commitment and arousing the enthusiasm of those who must
teach it.

Appendix

# KEY DOCUMENTS IN THE DEVELOPMENT OF GOVERNMENT POLICY ON THE CURRICULUM

*1. Department of Education and Science*

Prime Minister's Ruskin College Speech (1976) 'Towards a National Debate', printed in *Education* (22 October 1976), pp. 332–3

*Education in Schools: a consultative document*, 1977

*A Framework for the School Curriculum*, 1979

*The School Curriculum*, 1981

*Records of Achievement: a statement of policy*, 1984

*Better Schools* (White Paper), 1985

(with Department of Employment) *Education and Training for Young People* (White Paper), 1985

(with Department of Employment) *Working Together – Education and Training* (White Paper), 1986

*The National Curriculum: a consultative document*, 1987

*2. Her Majesty's Inspectorate*

Curriculum 11–16, 1977

Aspects of Secondary Education, 1979

Curriculum Matters Series 5–16

    1 English (1986)

    2 Curriculum (1985)

    3 Mathematics (1987)

    4 Music (1985)

    5 Home Economics (1985)

    6 Health Education (1986)

    7 Geography (1986)

8 Modern Foreign Languages (1986)
9 Craft, Design, and Technology (1987)
10 Careers Education and Guidance (1988)
11 History (1988)
12 Environmental Education (1989)

## 3. Government Committees of Enquiry

1974 Bullock Report, *A Language for Life*
1977 Taylor Report, *A New Partnership for our Schools*
1978 Warnock Report, *Special Educational Needs*
1982 Cockcroft Report, *Mathematics Counts*
1985 Swann Report, *Education for All*
1988 Kingman Report, *Teaching of English Language*

## 4. National Curriculum and Consultation Working Papers

1987 The National Curriculum 5–16 – a Consultation Document
National Curriculum: Task Group on Assessment and Testing – A Report
1988 National Curriculum: Task Group on Assessment and Testing – Three Supplementary Reports
Science for Ages 5 to 16 (Thompson Report)
Mathematics for Ages 5 to 16
English for Ages 5 to 11 (Cox Report)
Design and Technology 11–16 (Parker Report)
1989 National Curriculum: from Policy to Practice
The National Curriculum Information Pack No. 1

# INDEX